THE ZODIAC GUIDE TO LIVING

THE ZODIAC GUIDE TO LIVING

RODNEY DAVIES

BOXTREE

First published in Great Britain in 1993 by Boxtree Limited, Broadwall House, 21 Broadwall, London SE1 9PL

10 9 8 7 6 5 4 3 2 1

ISBN: 1 85283 551 6

Designed by Hammond and Hammond
Typeset by SX Composing Ltd.
Printed and bound in Great Britain by Cox and Wyman, Reading, Berkshire

A CIP catalogue entry for this book is available from the British Library

To my Mother: parent, friend, guide, and copy-reader.

Contents

THE TASK of an author is, either to teach what is not known, or to recommend known truths, by his manner of adorning them; either to let new light in upon the mind, and open new scenes to the prospect, or to vary the dress and situation of common objects, so as to give them fresh grace and more powerful attractions, to spread such flowers over the regions through which the intellect has already made its progress, as may tempt it to return, and take a second view of things hastily passed over or negligently regarded.

From *The Rambler No. 3* by Samuel Johnson

Introduction

THE WORD astrology means 'star study', yet although people have looked up at the heavens with awe and interest ever since they first walked the earth, the systematic observation of celestial objects and their movements did not take place until about 4,500 years ago.

The pioneer star-studiers or astrologers were the Sumerians, a people who lived in large brick-built cities sited on the banks of the lower reaches of the Tigris and Euphrates rivers, in what is now southern Iraq. They were not, however, disinterested observers of the starry firmament, for they and their fellow countrymen believed that the sky was the home of the gods. Indeed, the Sun, the Moon, and the 'wandering stars' or planets, were each thought to be the residence of a god or goddess, and the astrologers hoped that by watching them and the changes they underwent, in the form of eclipses, phases of the Moon, and conjunctions (or drawing together of the planets), they might determine the will of the gods, and so know how to better counsel their king. Hence early astrology was religious in nature, and its practitioners were essentially seekers of divine guidance.

Through such regular observation and by keeping careful records of what they saw, the star studiers soon discovered that both the Moon and the planets, and also, they later learned, the Sun, follow the same path, or ecliptic, through certain star groups or constellations. And because the latter were eventually all given animal names, it led to them being collectively named the zodiac, a word derived from the Greek *zodiakos*, meaning 'animal'.

We now recognise twelve zodiac constellations, which are popularly referred to as the signs of the zodiac. Their Latin names are Aries (the Ram), Taurus (the Bull), Gemini (the

Twins), Cancer (the Crab), Leo (the Lion), Virgo (the Virgin), Libra (the Balance), Scorpio (the Scorpion), Sagittarius (the Centaur), Capricorn (the Goat), Aquarius (the Water Pourer), and Pisces (the Fish).

When the Sumerian astrologers further discovered that the influence or 'will' of the astral deities was related to their position in the zodiac and to each other, it gave them the ability (once the movements of the Sun, the Moon, and the planets were understood and their future positions could be calculated) to foretell what good or bad happenings the gods were planning. This was the beginning of predictive astrology, an art which continues to be practised today, for while we no longer believe in the divinity of celestial objects, the idea and feeling persists that they somehow influence or symbolise our persons and our habits, and either determine or reflect our fate.

Astrology became applicable to the man-in-the-street when it was realised that every individual's personal characteristics and destiny is written in the stars at the moment of his or her birth. We do not know quite when this significant insight happened, but the drawing and interpreting of birth charts or horoscopes was certainly taking place by about 450 BC.

By using a system of correspondences, astrologers have linked the zodiac signs and their associated planets with all aspects of life on earth. Each is held to rule and thus perhaps control not only our emotional life, career prospects, likes and dislikes, and health, but also a whole range of objects, foods, substances, activities, and geographical areas, which are considered lucky or fortunate for those born under the zodiac sign in question.

This book is written to help all who wish to take advantage of this fact, for it explains what is good or beneficial for you, and what is bad or harmful, thereby giving you the opportunity to improve the quality of your life and to increase your luck.

And that is why its title is *The Zodiac Guide to Living*!

1

Knowing Your Signs

At my Nativity my Ascendant was the watery sign of Scorpius;
I was born in the Planetary hour of Saturn, and I think I have
a piece of that leaden Planet in me. I am no way facetious, nor
disposed for the mirth and galliardize of company; yet in one
dream I can compose a whole Comedy, behold the action,
apprehend the jests, and laugh my self awake at the conceits
thereof.

From *Religio Medici* by Sir Thomas Browne

THE ZODIAC signs which are of prime importance to you are:
(1) that which the Sun was passing through or transiting
when you were born, which is familiarly called your Sun sign,
and (2) that which was then rising or ascending above the
eastern horizon.

Your Sun Sign

You may already know your Sun sign. If you do not, you can
easily find out what it is from the table overleaf. However, if
you were born on one of the three days at the start or the end
of your zodiac sign period, you are a cuspal type, which means
you possess some of the looks and character traits linked with
the sign either preceding or following your own.

Those born on 21, 22, or 23 March, for example, have
Aries for their Sun sign, yet will share some features associated
with the preceding sign, Pisces, while those born on 18, 19 or
20 April, who likewise have an Aries Sun sign, will be in-
fluenced by the following sign, Taurus. These influences are

Born between	Your Sun sign is
21 March – 20 April	Aries, the Ram
21 April – 21 May	Taurus, the Bull
22 May – 21 June	Gemini, the Twins
22 June – 23 July	Cancer, the Crab
24 July – 23 August	Leo, the Lion
24 August – 23 September	Virgo, the Virgin
24 September – 22 October	Libra, the Balance
23 October – 22 November	Scorpio, the Scorpion
23 November – 22 December	Sagittarius, the Centaur
23 December – 20 January	Capricorn, the Goat
21 January – 19 February	Aquarius, the Water Pourer
20 February – 20 March	Pisces, the Fish

stronger the closer you are born to the dividing line or cusp between the signs.

Each of the zodiac signs is traditionally linked with one of the four ancient elements, these being Fire, Air, Earth, and Water. The Fire signs are Aries, Leo and Sagittarius; the Air signs are Gemini, Libra and Aquarius; the Earth signs are Taurus, Virgo and Capricorn; and the Water signs are Cancer, Scorpio and Pisces. These three-sign groupings are known technically as triplicities.

Fire sign people are typically outgoing, energetic, confident and ambitious; Air sign people tend to be unemotional, intelligent, independent and creative; Earth sign people are characteristically methodical, conservative, stubborn and practical; and Water sign people are typically caring, sympathetic, sensitive and artistic.

Just as in Nature a fire needs the oxygen contained in air to enable it to burn, and the air is correspondingly heated by fire and caused to rise, so Fire sign and Air sign individuals are generally compatible and mutually stimulating. Similarly, just as the earth provides a home for water, while at the same time being moistened and thus rendered life-giving by it, so Earth sign and Water sign people are generally compatible and mutually supportive.

Fire sign people, however, have little in common with Earth sign types, whom they find too slow and too lacking in enthusiasm to suit their get-up-and-go approach to life, and even less with Water sign types, whose uncertainty and want of drive has a naturally extinguishing effect on them. But while Air sign individuals also do not have much in common with Earth or Water sign types, their more patient and tolerant nature means that they are less irritated by them and are therefore rather more compatible with them.

Another way of grouping the zodiac signs is based on the position they occupy within the seasons of the year. The spring signs are Aries, Taurus and Gemini; the summer signs are Cancer, Leo and Virgo; the autumn signs are Libra, Scorpio and Sagittarius; and the winter signs are Capricorn, Aquarius and Pisces. Those placed at the start of a season, namely Aries, Cancer, Libra and Capricorn, are called *cardinal* signs; those placed in the middle of a season, namely Taurus, Leo, Scorpio and Aquarius, are known as *fixed* signs; and those situated at the end of a season, namely Gemini, Virgo, Sagittarius and Pisces, are called *mutable* signs. Astrologers refer to these four-sign groupings as quadruplicities.

The qualities associated with the cardinal signs, which derive from their place at the beginning of a season and so encompass notions of the first, are youthful enthusiasm, energy, confidence and enterprise. Those of the fixed signs, which are placed in the middle of a season when the weather conditions have stabilised, are caution, stability, thoughtfulness and reserve. Those of the mutable signs, placed at the end of a season when the conditions are again changing, are contrariness, adaptability, sociability and, frequently, instability.

This classification naturally modifies the qualities assigned to the triplicities. For example, a person born under Aries, a cardinal Fire sign, has the Fire sign qualities of extroversion, confidence and ambition developed to the full, to the extent of him or her often being brash and impatient, whereas the Leo individual, a fixed Fire type, is usually much more stable, responsible and dependable. The Sagittarian, being a mutable Fire sign type, often lacks the self-confidence and drive that distinguishes the two other Fire signs and this may hinder his or her career success, yet this type is the most sociable and self-indulgent of the three.

These seasonal placement character variations also apply to the Air, Earth, and Water sign triplicities. In fact they provide us with a scale that runs from Aries, a cardinal Fire sign, the most brash, pushy and outgoing zodiac type, to Pisces, a mutable Water sign, which is typically the shyest, most diffident and least emotionally-stable zodiac type.

Your Ruling Planets

The zodiac signs are ruled by one or other of the seven traditional astrological planets, these being the Sun, the Moon, Mercury, Venus, Mars, Jupiter and Saturn. The more recently discovered planets of Uranus, Neptune and Pluto have also been assigned rulerships, although these are still somewhat controversial. They are certainly ignored by astrologers in eastern countries. Your planetary ruler can be discovered from the list opposite.

The Sun represents the ego or the conscious mind, which is why its placement in the zodiac at the moment of birth is taken as an important guide to how a person thinks and behaves. Its zodiac position also reflects your appearance, colouring, and bearing. More generally, the Sun is said to govern the soul; your father and your relationship with him; the qualities of prestige and influence; the right eye, the heart, and the brain; royalty and royal favour; churches and other places of religious worship; prophecy; the metal gold and the colour gold; gemstones like the sardonyx; and the direction east. Because the Sun rules Leo, it accounts for the need of those born under this sign to be respected and looked up to, and always to be the centre of attention.

The Moon is the astral symbol of the unconscious mind and of the emotions, and thus of those deeper and more mysterious

Zodiac sign	Planetary ruler
Aries	Mars
Taurus	Venus
Gemini	Mercury
Cancer	the Moon
Leo	the Sun
Virgo	Mercury
Libra	Venus
Scorpio	Mars
Sagittarius	Jupiter
Capricorn	Saturn
Aquarius	Saturn
Pisces	Jupiter

areas of the human personality. It represents the home; pregnancy and childbirth; your mother and your relationship with her; the qualities of sensitivity and sympathy; intuition and psychic awareness; the left eye, the stomach, the lymph glands, the breasts, and the uterus; the sea and all places where water flows or is stored; the metal silver and all white or pale colours; gemstones like the ruby; and the direction northwest. As the ruler of Cancer, the Moon imparts to this sign the qualities of concern and caring, and an interest in parenthood and domesticity, which are so characteristic of the type.

Mercury is the indicator of intelligence, rationality, and speech and expression, thus it governs your mental powers and how you communicate. It also signifies childhood and youth; your maternal uncles and your relationship with them; your sense of humour; education and study; political leanings; interest in medicine, mathematics, astrology, and publishing; the hands, arms and shoulders, the lungs, the abdomen, and the nervous system; slimness and a high metabolic rate; deviousness and deception; sports and games and those places where they are played; the metal mercury and the colour yellow; gemstones like the agate; and the direction north. Mercury is the ruler of Gemini and Virgo, and gives to those born under these signs their characteristic loquacity and mental quickness, also their tendency to dissimulate, which mark them out.

Mars determines how you utilise your body energy, particularly how it is expressed as anger, courage, and ambition. It likewise signifies zeal and enthusiasm; your siblings and cousins and your relationship with them; manliness and martial prowess; physical strength; the nose and the right nostril, the head, the muscles, and the external genitalia; wounds and accidents; the army and police and places like barracks, armaments-manufacturers and stores, and factories where fire is used; the metal iron and the colour red; gemstones like the diamond; and the direction south-west. Because Mars rules Aries and Scorpio, it gives to those born under these signs a combative disposition, considerable courage, and a desire to succeed, but also a tendency to ride rough shod over others.

Venus is the prime signifier of sexual passion, of pleasure and of artistic interests. It is also believed to govern marriage and children; your wife and your relationship with her; femininity and peace; the left nostril, the throat, and the ovaries; venereal diseases; beauty parlours, brothels, and places like theatres and concert halls where acting, music and dance are performed; the metal copper and the colour green; gemstones like the emerald; and the direction south-east. Venus rules the zodiac signs of Taurus and Libra, and gives to those born under them their characteristic qualities of reasonableness and good temper, and their talent and liking for music and art.

Jupiter is the planet that controls, on the one hand, the higher development of the mind, being the signifier of wisdom, honesty, truth, deep study and reflection, and on the other, the taste and appetite for food and drink. It governs wealth and institutions like banks and mints; your husband and your relationship with him; qualities like generosity and fairness; philosophy and religion; hotels and restaurants; legal affairs; governments and ministers; the right ear, the thighs, the feet, the kidneys, fatty deposits, and the arteries and veins; the gaining of respect; the metal tin and the colour purple; gemstones like the turquoise; and the direction north-east. As the ruler of Sagittarius and Pisces, it imparts to those born under them a love of equity and fair-play, a sociable nature, but also their tendency to over-indulge themselves.

Saturn is both the controller of bodily stasis, thereby potentially bringing about your survival into old age, and the determinator of qualities like reserve and reflection. It is also the ruler of your servants and employees and your relationship with them; agriculture and mineral exploration and extraction; places of incarceration like prisons and asylums; rubbish tips and crematoria; architecture and building; regret and disillusion; the left ear, the bones, the skin, the spleen, and the knees and lower legs; skill at learning foreign languages; the metal lead and the colour black; gemstones like the garnet; and the direction west. In the zodiac Saturn rules Capricorn and Aquarius, and gives to those born under them their characteristic caution and sagacity, and their interest in unknown things, but also their despondency.

Your Ascending Sign

In addition to your Sun sign and your ruling planet, it is also necessary for you to know which zodiac sign was rising (or ascending) above the horizon at the time of your birth. The importance of this sign is considerable for it not only helps determine, or at least signify, your appearance, but also a good deal of your personality and inherent talent, which is why most astrologers rank it equal to the Sun sign in this regard. Some rate it even higher.

If you know the time of your birth, even if only approximately, the tables on the next three pages will enable you to quickly discover your ascendant. However, do remember that if you were born in Great Britain during the spring, summer or early autumn, when Summer Time is in operation, you must deduct one hour from your birth time to convert it to Greenwich Mean Time or GMT. Since 1975 Summer Time has started at 2 a.m. on the third Sunday in March and ended at 2 a.m. on the fourth Sunday in October. Prior to 1975 the

ARIES

Time of birth	Ascendant
Midnight – 2 a.m.	Capricorn
2 a.m. – 4 a.m.	Aquarius
4 a.m. – 6 a.m.	Pisces
6 a.m. – 8 a.m.	Aries
8 a.m. – 10 a.m.	Taurus
10 a.m. – Noon	Gemini
Noon – 2 p.m.	Cancer
2 p.m. – 4 p.m.	Leo
4 p.m. – 6 p.m.	Virgo
6 p.m. – 8 p.m.	Libra
8 p.m. – 10 p.m.	Scorpio
10 p.m. – Midnight	Sagittarius

TAURUS

Time of birth	Ascendant
Midnight – 2 a.m.	Aquarius
2 a.m. – 4 a.m.	Pisces
4 a.m. – 6 a.m.	Aries
6 a.m. – 8 a.m.	Taurus
8 a.m. – 10 a.m.	Gemini
10 a.m. – Noon	Cancer
Noon – 2 p.m.	Leo
2 p.m. – 4 p.m.	Virgo
4 p.m. – 6 p.m.	Libra
6 p.m. – 8 p.m.	Scorpio
8 p.m. – 10 p.m.	Sagittarius
10 p.m. – Midnight	Capricorn

GEMINI

Time of birth	Ascendant
Midnight – 2 a.m.	Pisces
2 a.m. – 4 a.m.	Aries
4 a.m. – 6 a.m.	Taurus
6 a.m. – 8 a.m.	Gemini
8 a.m. – 10 a.m.	Cancer
10 a.m. – Noon	Leo
Noon – 2 p.m.	Virgo
2 p.m. – 4 p.m.	Libra
4 p.m. – 6 p.m.	Scorpio
6 p.m. – 8 p.m.	Sagittarius
8 p.m. – 10 p.m.	Capricorn
10 p.m. – Midnight	Aquarius

CANCER

Time of birth	Ascendant
Midnight – 2 a.m.	Aries
2 a.m. – 4 a.m.	Taurus
4 a.m. – 6 a.m.	Gemini
6 a.m. – 8 a.m.	Cancer
8 a.m. – 10 a.m.	Leo
10 a.m. – Noon	Virgo
Noon – 2 p.m.	Libra
2 p.m. – 4 p.m.	Scorpio
4 p.m. – 6 p.m.	Sagittarius
6 p.m. – 8 p.m.	Capricorn
8 p.m. – 10 p.m.	Aquarius
10 p.m. – Midnight	Pisces

dates for the beginning and end of the Summer Time period varied from year to year. The table on pages 11 and 12 shows exactly when the clocks were moved forward and backwards.

People who were born during this period in World War II, will have to deduct two hours from their birth time as Double

LEO

Time of birth	Ascendant
Midnight – 2 a.m.	Taurus
2 a.m. – 4 a.m.	Gemini
4 a.m. – 6 a.m.	Cancer
6 a.m. – 8 a.m.	Leo
8 a.m. – 10 a.m.	Virgo
10 a.m. – Noon	Libra
Noon – 2 p.m.	Scorpio
2 p.m. – 4 p.m.	Sagittarius
4 p.m. – 6 p.m.	Capricorn
6 p.m. – 8 p.m.	Aquarius
8 p.m. – 10 p.m.	Pisces
10 p.m. – Midnight	Aries

VIRGO

Time of birth	Ascendant
Midnight – 2 a.m.	Gemini
2 a.m. – 4 a.m.	Cancer
4 a.m. – 6 a.m.	Leo
6 a.m. – 8 a.m.	Virgo
8 a.m. – 10 a.m.	Libra
10 a.m. – Noon	Scorpio
Noon – 2 p.m.	Sagittarius
2 p.m. – 4 p.m.	Capricorn
4 p.m. – 6 p.m.	Aquarius
6 p.m. – 8 p.m.	Pisces
8 p.m. – 10 p.m.	Aries
10 p.m. – Midnight	Taurus

LIBRA

Time of birth	Ascendant
Midnight – 2 a.m.	Cancer
2 a.m. – 4 a.m.	Leo
4 a.m. – 6 a.m.	Virgo
6 a.m. – 8 a.m.	Libra
8 a.m. – 10 a.m.	Scorpio
10 a.m. – Noon	Sagittarius
Noon – 2 p.m.	Capricorn
2 p.m. – 4 p.m.	Aquarius
4 p.m. – 6 p.m.	Pisces
6 p.m. – 8 p.m.	Aries
8 p.m. – 10 p.m.	Taurus
10 p.m. – Midnight	Gemini

SCORPIO

Time of birth	Ascendant
Midnight – 2 a.m.	Leo
2 a.m. – 4 a.m.	Virgo
4 a.m. – 6 a.m.	Libra
6 a.m. – 8 a.m.	Scorpio
8 a.m. – 10 a.m.	Sagittarius
10 a.m. – Noon	Capricorn
Noon – 2 p.m.	Aquarius
2 p.m. – 4 p.m.	Pisces
4 p.m. – 6 p.m.	Aries
6 p.m. – 8 p.m.	Taurus
8 p.m. – 10 p.m.	Gemini
10 p.m. – Midnight	Cancer

Summer Time was then in operation, while those born during the rest of the year need to deduct one hour owing to the year-long employment of Summer Time. An experimental Summer Time period was also in operation between 18 February 1968 and 31 October 1971. People born at any time of the year

SAGITTARIUS		CAPRICORN	
Time of birth	*Ascendant*	*Time of birth*	*Ascendant*
Midnight – 2 a.m.	Virgo	Midnight – 2 a.m.	Libra
2 a.m. – 4 a.m.	Libra	2 a.m. – 4 a.m.	Scorpio
4 a.m. – 6 a.m.	Scorpio	4 a.m. – 6 a.m.	Sagittarius
6 a.m. – 8 a.m.	Sagittarius	6 a.m. – 8 a.m.	Capricorn
8 a.m. – 10 a.m.	Capricorn	8 a.m. – 10 a.m.	Aquarius
10 a.m. – Noon	Aquarius	10 a.m. – Noon	Pisces
Noon – 2 p.m.	Pisces	Noon – 2 p.m.	Aries
2 p.m. – 4 p.m.	Aries	2 p.m. – 4 p.m.	Taurus
4 p.m. – 6 p.m.	Taurus	4 p.m. – 6 p.m.	Gemini
6 p.m. – 8 p.m.	Gemini	6 p.m. – 8 p.m.	Cancer
8 p.m. – 10 p.m.	Cancer	8 p.m. – 10 p.m.	Leo
10 p.m. – Midnight	Leo	10 p.m. – Midnight	Virgo

AQUARIUS		PISCES	
Time of birth	*Ascendant*	*Time of birth*	*Ascendant*
Midnight – 2 a.m.	Scorpio	Midnight – 2 a.m.	Sagittarius
2 a.m. – 4 a.m.	Sagittarius	2 a.m. – 4 a.m.	Capricorn
4 a.m. – 6 a.m.	Capricorn	4 a.m. – 6 a.m.	Aquarius
6 a.m. – 8 a.m.	Aquarius	6 a.m. – 8 a.m.	Pisces
8 a.m. – 10 a.m.	Pisces	8 a.m. – 10 a.m.	Aries
10 a.m. – Noon	Aries	10 a.m. – Noon	Taurus
Noon – 2 p.m.	Taurus	Noon – 2 p.m.	Gemini
2 p.m. – 4 p.m.	Gemini	2 p.m. – 4 p.m.	Cancer
4 p.m. – 6 p.m.	Cancer	4 p.m. – 6 p.m.	Leo
6 p.m. – 8 p.m.	Leo	6 p.m. – 8 p.m.	Virgo
8 p.m. – 10 p.m.	Virgo	8 p.m. – 10 p.m.	Libra
10 p.m. – Midnight	Libra	10 p.m. – Midnight	Scorpio

between these two dates must subtract one hour from their birth time before consulting the tables.

Because the tables are based on a sunrise time of 6 a.m. GMT, they cannot be accurate for everyone, due to the fact that the time the Sun rises changes constantly as the year goes by.

	Summer Time	Double Summer Time
1916	21 May to 1 October	
1917	8 April to 17 September	
1918	24 March to 30 September	
1919	30 March to 29 September	
1920	28 March to 25 October	
1921	3 April to 3 October	
1922	26 March to 8 October	
1923	22 April to 16 September	
1924	13 April to 21 September	
1925	19 April to 4 October	
1926	18 April to 3 October	
1927	10 April to 2 October	
1928	22 April to 7 October	
1929	21 April to 6 October	
1930	13 April to 5 October	
1931	19 April to 4 October	
1932	17 April to 2 October	
1933	9 April to 8 October	
1934	22 April to 7 October	
1935	14 April to 6 October	
1936	19 April to 4 October	
1937	18 April to 3 October	
1938	10 April to 2 October	
1939	16 April to 19 November	
1940	25 February to 31 December	
1941	1 January to 31 December	4 May to 10 August
1942	1 January to 31 December	5 April to 9 August
1943	1 January to 31 December	4 April to 15 August
1944	1 January to 31 December	2 April to 17 Sept
1945	1 January to 7 October	2 April to 15 July
1946	14 April to 6 October	
1947	16 March to 2 November	13 April to 10 August
1948	14 March to 31 October	
1949	3 April to 30 October	
1950	16 April to 22 October	

	Summer Time	**Double Summer Time**
1951	15 April to 21 October	
1952	20 April to 26 October	
1953	19 April to 4 October	
1954	11 April to 3 October	
1955	17 April to 2 October	
1956	22 April to 7 October	
1957	14 April to 6 October	
1958	20 April to 5 October	
1959	19 April to 5 October	
1960	10 April to 2 October	
1961	26 March to 29 October	
1962	25 March to 28 October	
1963	31 March to 27 October	
1964	22 March to 25 March	
1965	21 March to 24 October	
1966	20 March to 23 October	
1967	19 March to 29 October	
1968	18 February	
1969		
1970	to	Experimental Summer Time Period
1971	31 October	
1972	19 March to 29 October	
1973	18 March to 28 October	
1974	17 March to 27 October	

So if you were born, say, in Great Britain during the summer, when the Sun can rise as early as 3.45 a.m. GMT, the sign preceding the one given below for your two-hour birth time period may well be your ascendant. If you were born during the winter, when the Sun can rise as late as 8.05 a.m., your ascending sign may be the one following that given below for your two-hour birth time period. If you were not born in Great Britain remember to convert your birth time to GMT.

If you were born in Great Britain during the two-hour

period between 6 a.m. and 8 a.m., your ascending sign is the same as your Sun sign (although don't forget to make the same sign adjustment as that mentioned above if you were born in either the winter or summer). This makes you a double Aquarius, a double Scorpio or double whichever sign, and your physical type and character will fully accord with that ascribed to the sign in question. But if your Sun sign and ascending sign are different, you will be something of a blend of two signs, although perhaps in certain areas one sign may predominate. This is why you should read what is said about both signs, and both planetary rulers, in the remainder of the book.

2

Food and Dieting

Nature delights in the most plain and simple diet. Every animal but man keeps to one dish. Herbs are the food of this species, fish of that, and flesh of a third. Man falls upon everything that comes in his way; not the smallest fruit or excrescence of the earth, scarce a berry or a mushroom, can escape him.

From *The Spectator No. 195* by Joseph Addison

WE MUST all eat to live, and nowadays we recognise that a healthy diet is the best way not only to feel well, but to prevent those degenerative diseases that are caused or exacerbated by the ingestion of too much fat and sugar.

Yet while we in the West are fortunate in having plentiful supplies of cheap food, the danger of such abundance is that many people eat too much and become overweight, which not only causes them anxiety about their appearance but ironically exposes them to health hazards in the form of heart attacks and strokes.

A healthy diet is one that provides us with sufficient protein, carbohydrate, fat, fibre, mineral salts and vitamins to allow our bodies to function at an optimum level. The first four components, unlike the last two, are required in relatively large amounts, although all are essential for good health.

However, a lot of people are puzzled to find that, despite trying to eat sensibly and moderately, they are either left unsatisfied by what they consume or they gain unwanted weight, while others who eat heartily and with relish gain no weight at all.

The answer to this apparent conundrum is that the internal environment of our bodies varies, rather like our tastes, so that what one person finds enjoyable, satisfying to eat and easily digestible, often has quite the opposite effect on another. Not only do our digestive processes and their efficiency differ, but also our metabolic rates and the ease or readiness with which we store fat. At worst, certain foods may so negatively affect the internal environment of some people that they cause allergic reactions, which may in turn prompt debilitating migraine headaches.

Ideally then, you need to eat those foods that are most compatible with your biochemical nature, while avoiding those that are not. The best guide to what foods are compatible with you is provided by the planetary ruler of your Sun sign. This governs those types of foodstuff that are harmonious with your body and with all others born under that particular zodiac sign.

The foods linked with each plant are shown below:

The Sun (rules Leo): because it provides the light and warmth needed for plant growth, the Sun powers the food chain and is therefore associated with each food type. Yet it is particularly said to rule apples and most yellow or orange-coloured citrus fruits, such as nectarines, oranges, tangerines, lemons and grapefruit, as well as grapes (and hence currants, raisins and sultanas) and vegetables like yams and sweet potatoes. It is also the ruler of rice. Because it governs the cockerel, the Sun has lordship over the supermarket capon; it also rules over the flesh of the heart. The culinary herbs and spices ruled by the Sun are angelica, bay leaves, camomile, cinnamon, cloves, rosemary and saffron; it is also the co-ruler, along with the Moon, of vinegar. Sunflower seeds, as might be expected, are governed by the Sun, as are sunflower oil and margarine. The Sun's liquids include orange juice, grapefruit juice and other citrus drinks, including squashes, cider, and tea. While the Sun has general rulership over all wines, this capacity is shared, according to the wine type, with the Moon, Mercury, and Mars.

The Moon (rules Cancer): most vegetables with a high water content are ruled by the Moon; these include cabbage, cauliflower, celery, cucumber, leek, lettuce, marrow, melon, pumpkin, watercress, and watermelon. White or pale-coloured vegetables like parsnips, turnips and shallots are also ruled by the Moon (although some astrologers would attribute white beets to Jupiter). Milk products like cheese, yoghurt, butter and cream are governed by the Moon. Tripe comes under the Moon's rulership, as well as all fresh water fish, such as salmon, tench, and bream, and, along with Neptune, all sea fish, including tuna, pilchards, kippers, sardines, eels, octopus, also shellfish (e.g. oysters, whelks, cockles, shrimps, prawns, crabs and lobsters); fish paste, fish oil, caviare and other fish products; turtle soup; seaweed and kelp. The Moon's spice is salt. Ginseng is also governed by the Moon, as is chocolate. Its liquids include water, especially spring water, colourless soft drinks, milk (but not goat's milk), hot chocolate, and white wine.

Mercury (rules Gemini and Virgo): the meat of all birds with the exception of the capon and game birds is governed by this planet, which naturally includes chicken, duck, goose and turkey. Eggs and bird innards like goose liver, used in pâté de foie gras, similarly animal's brains, tongues and lights or lungs come under the rulership of Mercury. Likewise all leguminous vegetables, such as peas, French beans, runner beans, haricot beans and broad beans (although some astrologers assign beans to Venus) are Mercury's subjects, as are many nuts, including hazel nuts, almonds and coconuts; carrots, ladyfingers (okra), mushrooms and all non-cereal seeds are governed by Mercury. Pomegranates and mulberries are also ruled by Mercury. Its culinary herbs and spices are calamint, caraway, dill, fenugreek, marjoram and parsley. The laxative senna is likewise ruled by Mercury, as are all aerated drinks, including sparkling wines.

Venus (rules Taurus and Libra): the planet of love was once a vegetation goddess, so it is not surprising that Venus has rulership over most non-citrus fruits, such as apricots, bananas, blackberries, cherries, gooseberries, guavas, lychees, mangoes, peaches, pears, pineapples, plums, raspberries and strawberries; cereals like wheat, oats and rye (but not barley and rice), and hence flour and starch, bread and bread products, cakes and buns, and pasta; and certain vegetables like courgettes, lentils, sweet corn, and green peppers. The principal animal edible Venus rules is kidney. Sugar and artificial sweeteners like saccharin are also governed by Venus, as are honey, syrup and molasses. The planet's culinary herbs are mint, pennyroyal, sorrel and thyme, and its liquids are noncitrus fruit juices, mead, plum wine and elderberry wine, alcoholic drinks made from grains, such as whisky and rye, as well as rum, sherry, port and sweet liqueurs.

Mars (rules Aries and Scorpio): the red planet has governance over most types of meat, notably beef, pork, mutton, lamb, veal and horse flesh; many, but not all, vegetables that are coloured red, such as tomatoes, horseradishes, red cabbage, red peppers, and many red-coloured fruits and berries with the exception of those ruled by Venus, e.g. cranberries, red currants, black currants, and rhubarb. Mars rules basil and vanilla and those culinary herbs and spices that are hot, such as cayenne pepper, chives, chilli powder, euphorbia, garlic, mustard, ordinary pepper, and onions. It rules spinach and also the nettle plant, from which a pleasant tea and wine can be made, two of the liquids governed by Mars. The others are coffee, beer, lager, and red wine.

Jupiter (rules Sagittarius and Pisces): the number of foodstuffs ruled over by the largest of the planets is surprisingly small and restricted. Where meat is concerned, for example, Jupiter is given jurisdiction only over those obtained from game animals, the co-ruled 'royal' meats, such as venison, antelope, boar and moose, and over game birds like grouse, pheasant, ptarmigan and quail. However, it does rule all animal liver (except that obtained from birds), and fats. The fruits ruled by Jupiter are the bilberry (or whortleberry), the fig and the lime. Where common vegetables are concerned, Jupiter has dominion only over asparagus, the endive and the olive (and hence olive oil), although Culpeper also gives it rulership over white beets, such as parsnips, turnips and sugar beet. Maple syrup is governed by Jupiter, as is the humble but useful dandelion plant, whose leaves can be eaten as a salad vegetable, its flowers brewed into wine, and its roots made into a coffee. Jupiter's nut is the sweet chestnut, and its culinary herbs and spices are balm, chervil, nutmeg, mace and sage. Its alcoholic drinks include dandelion wine, absinthe and anisette liqueur.

Saturn (rules Capricorn and Aquarius): the last of the traditional planets also rules a rather limited range of foodstuffs, of which some, notably those meats that are hung up to mature, are co-ruled by Jupiter, e.g. pheasant. Goat's meat, however, is ruled by Saturn alone, as is goat's milk. It similarly shares governance with Pluto over those fungi like truffles that grow underground, and of most subterranean vegetables, such as potatoes, celeriac, chicory, kohlrabi, radishes, salsify, swedes, Jerusalem artichokes, scorzonera, and sea-kale beets, Chilean beets and other red beets. The cereal barley is also ruled by Saturn, as is the aubergine or egg-plant. Certain of the fruits governed by the planet are dark-coloured, such as medlars and sloes, but others, like the quince, are not. Saturn rules the beech nut and the peanut, and its liquids include barley water, ordinary gin and sloe gin, and all alcoholic potato-based drinks, such as vodka.

The general rule where nutrition and your diet are concerned, is that you should eat those foods governed by your planetary ruler, plus those belonging to the other two signs of its triplicity. Hence if you were born, for example, under Scorpio, which belongs to the Water triplicity, ideally your food choices should be from those listed under the rulership of Mars (Scorpio's ruler), along with those ruled by the Moon (Cancer) and Jupiter (Pisces). You will probably find these foods to be the most tasty and acceptable. The types of food governed by these three planets or signs are many and varied, and will provide you with a sufficiently wide choice to enable you to eat both soundly and well. The same is generally true no matter what sign you were born under.

If you need more variety, you will find that the foods governed by the planetary ruler of your rising sign (or ascendant) are also appealing to you and compatible with you. Indeed, if you have the same Sun sign and ascending sign, you will particularly like and benefit from the foods associated with it. And if you are a cuspal type you will also like those foods associated with the adjacent zodiac sign, which will in general be quite compatible with you.

The same rule applies when eating dishes made with several ingredients. The most enjoyable recipes and the best ones for you contain ingredients that are compatible with your zodiac nature.

Some foods ruled by other planets may disagree with you to the extent of causing digestive upset, stomach ache or flatulence, and should be avoided, although most will probably not harm you and can be eaten and enjoyed at least occasionally. So use your common sense when deciding upon what to eat and do not be overly strict with yourself.

The table overleaf shows you from which of the previously mentioned planet lists to choose your basic diet, according to your Sun sign.

Those born under the Earth triplicity of Taurus, Virgo and Capricorn, and the Air triplicity of Gemini, Libra and Aquarius, have the same planetary food lists from which to choose, namely those of Venus, Mercury and Saturn, although in a different order of importance, preference and compatibility. These planets govern many of the most health-giving and nutritious foods, namely bread, pasta, potatoes, green vegetables (especially legumes), many fruits, low-fat fowl meat, nuts and seeds. It is therefore perhaps not surprising to find that five of the sign types, i.e. those born under Virgo, Capricorn, Gemini, Libra, and Aquarius, seldom have much trouble with their weight, and that women born under Gemini, Capricorn, Taurus and Libra live on average to be at least 75 years old, as do men born under the signs of Taurus and Capricorn. Indeed, were it not for the sweet tooth often encouraged among them by Venus, it is probable that they would all be slim, healthy and long-lived.

Zodiac sign	Food-indicating planets	
	Primary	*Secondary*
Aries	Mars	the Sun, Jupiter
Taurus	Venus	Mercury, Saturn
Gemini	Mercury	Venus, Saturn
Cancer	the Moon	Mars, Jupiter
Leo	the Sun	Jupiter, Mars
Virgo	Mercury	Venus, Saturn
Libra	Venus	Mercury, Saturn
Scorpio	Mars	Jupiter, the Moon
Sagittarius	Jupiter	Mars, the Sun
Capricorn	Saturn	Venus, Mercury
Aquarius	Saturn	Mercury, Venus
Pisces	Jupiter	the Moon, Mars

Yet the diets recommended for and preferred by those belonging to the Fire and the Water triplicities are no less healthy. Men born under Aries are the second longest-lived male zodiac type, trailing Taurus, while Aries women are the third longest-lived female zodiac type, coming after Gemini and Capricorn.

However, the meats ruled by Mars, favoured by those born under the Fire and Water signs, and the milk and milk products ruled by the Moon, do have a high fat content. The wise eater will therefore choose the lean meat cuts or remove any fat, and will drink semi-skimmed or skimmed milk and eat only low-fat dairy products. On the plus side, the low-fat Moon-ruled fish and fish products provide a valuable and nutritious protein source, and both the Moon-ruled and the Mars-ruled fruits and vegetables are very healthy to eat, especially when consumed fresh.

The Aries, Leo and Sagittarius-born may all eat the wide selection of foods ruled by the Sun, of which the citrus fruits and rice, along with the other grains (co-ruled by Venus), are perhaps the most valuable, while the Scorpio-born can widen their diet by eating those foods, like potatoes, governed by their co-ruler Pluto. The self-indulgent influence of Jupiter on the tastes and appetites of these six sign types, however, is perhaps the main reasons why three of them, namely Sagittarius, Cancer and Scorpio, lie towards the bottom end of the longevity scale for both sexes. The advice given by the Apollonian mottoes should thus be remembered and heeded by those born under these signs: 'All things in moderation' and 'Avoid excess'.

The following sample daily menus for each zodiac sign should give you some assistance in planning your own. They feature, where practicable, only those foods and drinks ruled by the planets forming the triplicity to which the sign belongs, and should prove both tasty and satisfying for those born under them.

ARIES (Mars, the Sun, Jupiter):

BREAKFAST: Half a grapefruit
Fried liver or bacon, onions and tomatoes, 1 slice of wholemeal bread with marmalade
Coffee

LUNCH: Bowl of chilli with rice
Fresh grapes
Coffee

DINNER: Minestrone soup
Spinach lasagne (made with spinach pasta)
Rhubarb crumble
1 glass of red wine or beer

SNACK: 1 orange

TAURUS (Venus, Mercury, Saturn):

BREAKFAST: Porridge or cornflakes served with semi-skimmed milk

1 slice of wholemeal toast with raspberry jam; tea

LUNCH: Spaghetti on wholemeal toast
Fresh fruit salad
Perrier water

DINNER: 1 glass of sherry as aperitif
Flambé kidneys, parsley noodles and green peas
Gooseberry tart with custard

SNACK: 1 peach or pear

GEMINI (Mercury, Venus, Saturn):

BREAKFAST: 1 poached egg on wholemeal toast
1 slice of wholemeal toast with strawberry jam
Lemon tea

LUNCH: Vegetable soup with noodles
Baked beans on wholemeal toast
Perrier water

DINNER: 1 glass of sherry as aperitif
Pea soup
Breaded veal cutlets, mashed potatoes with parsley, and mushrooms
Pear compôte
1 glass of sparkling wine

SNACK: 1 peach or some plums

CANCER (the Moon, Mars, Jupiter):

BREAKFAST: Porridge with added pinch of salt and served with semi-skimmed milk
Coffee

LUNCH: Poached halibut with white sauce, scalloped potatoes, and watercress
Natural yoghurt with added dash of

maple syrup
Mineral water; coffee

DINNER: Onion soup
Mixed liver-and-bacon grill, rice and lettuce, cucumber and tomato salad *or* cauliflower cheese
Custard tart with nutmeg
1 glass of white wine

SNACK: Walnuts or sweet chestnuts

LEO (the Sun, Jupiter, Mars):

BREAKFAST: Half a grapefruit
Bowl of rice cereal with semi-skimmed milk
1 slice of wholemeal toast with marmalade
Tea

LUNCH: Roasted lambs' hearts stuffed with rice and raisins, served with fried sweet potatoes *or* chicory (or endive) and pepper salad, served with cheese if desired
1 glass of cider or apple juice

DINNER: Ox-tail soup
Liver and apple casserole, mashed potatoes, mustard and spinach
Rice pudding
1 glass of red wine

SNACK: 1 orange or grapes

VIRGO (Mercury, Saturn, Venus):

BREAKFAST: 1 poached egg on wholemeal toast
1 slice of wholemeal toast with raspberry jam
Herbal tea

LUNCH: Mushroom omelette with green peas
Cherry and almond pie
Perrier water

DINNER: 1 glass of sherry as aperitif
Pâté de foie gras with hot toast and
butter *or* tabbouleh
Chicken croquettes, new potatoes and
carrots
Apricots or peaches and cream
1 glass of sparkling wine

SNACK: Hazel nuts or peanuts

LIBRA (Venus, Saturn, Mercury):

BREAKFAST: Cornflakes with semi-skimmed milk
1 slice of wholemeal toast and plum jam
Herbal tea

LUNCH: Tinned spaghetti on wholemeal toast
1 peach or pear
Perrier water

DINNER: 1 glass of sherry as aperitif
Carrot soup
Kidney omelette, chips and pepper salad
or lentil moussaka
Fruit snow
1 glass of sparkling wine

SNACK: 1 slice of sponge cake

SCORPIO (Mars, Jupiter, the Moon):

BREAKFAST: Fried bacon, sausage and tomatoes
1 slice of wholemeal toast
Coffee

LUNCH: Tuna fish casserole
Small dish of junket
1 glass of cranberry juice; coffee

DINNER: Cream of tomato soup
Hamburger meat balls with sour cream
and chopped chives, small serving of
chips, and asparagus
Blackcurrant pie with custard
1 glass of red wine

SNACK: Cheese and crackers

SAGITTARIUS (Jupiter, the Sun, Mars):

BREAKFAST: 1 glass of orange juice
Fried sausages with fried bread
Tea or coffee

LUNCH: Roast beef sandwich
Fresh fruit salad
1 glass of lime juice; coffee

DINNER: Chestnut soup
Chilli con carne with spinach salad
Apple crumble
1 glass of red wine or beer

SNACK: 1 orange or apple

CAPRICORN (Saturn, Venus, Mercury):

BREAKFAST: Cereal with semi-skimmed milk
1 slice of wholemeal toast with raspberry
jam
Herbal tea

LUNCH: Potato omelette with fried aubergines
1 peach or pear
1 glass of barley water

DINNER: 1 vodka or sherry as aperitif
Chicken consommé
Spaghetti bolognese
Fruit Charlotte
1 glass of red wine

SNACK: Peanuts or dried fruit

AQUARIUS (Saturn, Mercury, Venus):

BREAKFAST: 1 poached egg on wholemeal toast
              1 slice of wholemeal toast with plum jam
              Herbal tea

LUNCH: Peanut butter sandwich *or* celeriac and
              egg salad
              1 banana
              1 glass of barley water

DINNER: Vichyssoise
              Breaded chicken breasts, mashed
              potatoes with parsley, and fried
              aubergines
              Cherry and almond pie
              1 glass of sparkling wine

SNACK: Mixed nuts and dried fruit

PISCES (Jupiter, the Moon, Mars):

BREAKFAST: 2 kippers
              1 slice of wholemeal toast
              Coffee

LUNCH: Cheese and ham pudding with creamed
              spinach
              Mineral water

DINNER: Cold asparagus soup
              Pepper steak, small portion of creamed
              potatoes, and green salad
              Lime jelly and cream
              1 glass of red wine; coffee

SNACK: Olives with wholemeal bread
              Milk

The fixed signs of Taurus, Leo, Scorpio, and Aquarius, have,
as their quadruplicity name suggests, the least problem as far

as unwanted weight gain is concerned. They are the most emotionally stable of the twelve sign types, and thus are less prone to depressive bingeing or to ordinary self-indulgence than are the others, although Taureans may have most difficulty staying slim due to their love of good food and socialising. The fixed sign types are further helped in this regard by their metabolism, which deals efficiently with ingested calories and which builds up fat deposits slowly. However, they do need to be careful about avoiding long-term weight gain, as once fat has been accumulated they may find it difficult to slim.

The remaining eight signs have far more trouble in maintaining a constant weight, as they tend to add or lose pounds quite readily, although the rulership by Jupiter of Sagittarius and Pisces gives rise to the self-indulgence and 'well-covered' obesity, especially in middle-age, of those born under them. The activity (nervous or otherwise) and poor appetites of certain of them, notably Geminis and Virgos, helps them to burn off any excess energy or fat and thus remain slim in their youth, but once they reach 30 years and become more self-indulgent and less active, they may start to have problems with their girth and weight.

If your weight is more than you would like it to be and you feel you do need to diet, please understand that dieting can be successful only if you are resolute. Your diet must, in other words, be kept to, often over a period of several weeks or even months, while the weight is lost. Subsequently a new and lower calorie intake level must be adhered to indefinitely. Although this may be difficult for you, you can gain useful help from the zodiac, as the tables on the following two pages reveal. The first tells you the two zodiac periods during which you are most likely to gain weight, and have difficulty curbing your appetite, while the second shows the two zodiac periods when you can most easily lose weight, and which are therefore best for dieting.

These periods of easy gain or loss of weight reflect the changing influence of the Sun (and the Moon) on the hundreds of millions of cells that compose our bodies and which

1 *Zodiac sign*	*Zodiac periods when weight is gained easily*
Aries	Cancer (22 June – 23 July); Virgo (24 August – 23 September)
Taurus	Leo (24 July – 23 August); Libra (24 September – 22 October)
Gemini	Virgo (24 August – 23 September); Scorpio (23 October – 22 November)
Cancer	Libra (24 September – 22 October); Sagittarius (23 November – 22 December)
Leo	Scorpio (23 October – 22 November); Capricorn (23 December – 20 January)
Virgo	Sagittarius (23 November – 22 December); Aquarius (21 January – 19 February)
Libra	Capricorn (23 December – 20 January); Pisces (20 February – 20 March)
Scorpio	Aries (21 March – 20 April); Aquarius (21 January – 19 February)
Sagittarius	Pisces (20 February – 20 March); Taurus (21 April – 21 May)
Capricorn	Aries (21 March – 20 April); Gemini (22 May – 21 June)
Aquarius	Taurus (21 April – 21 May); Cancer (22 June – 23 July)
Pisces	Gemini (22 May – 21 June); Leo (24 July – 23 August)

act like miniature chemical factories. All the many and varied processes of life take place within these tiny enclosures, which are sensitive to both the positional placements in the zodiac of the Sun and the Moon, and to the electromagnetic and ion changes in the atmosphere caused by sunspots and solar flares.

2 *Zodiac sign*	*Zodiac periods when weight is lost easily*
Aries	Pisces (20 February – 20 March); Sagittarius (23 November – 22 December)
Taurus	Aries (21 March – 20 April); Capricorn (23 December – 20 January)
Gemini	Aquarius (21 January – 19 February); Taurus (21 April – 21 May)
Cancer	Pisces (20 February – 20 March); Gemini (22 June – 23 July)
Leo	Aries (21 March – 20 April); Cancer (22 June – 23 July)
Virgo	Taurus (21 April – 21 May); Leo (24 July – 23 August)
Libra	Gemini (22 May – 21 June); Virgo (24 August – 23 September)
Scorpio	Cancer (22 June – 23 July); Libra (24 September – 22 October)
Sagittarius	Leo (24 July – 23 August); Scorpio (23 October – 22 November)
Capricorn	Virgo (24 August – 23 September) Sagittarius (23 November – 22 December)
Aquarius	Libra (24 September – 22 October); Capricorn (23 December – 20 January)
Pisces	Scorpio (23 October – 22 November); Aquarius (21 January – 19 February)

The Moon, having as it does rulership over the stomach, controls our appetite. The latter tends to increase when the Moon is waxing (changing from New to Full), and to decrease when the Moon is waning (changing from Full to New), both periods taking about 14.75 days and together forming the lunar or synodial month of 29 days, 12 hours and 44 minutes. Hence extra care is required when there is a waxing Moon in order to prevent yourself from over-eating then and so taking in unwanted calories, whereas you can begin a diet with greater confidence at Full Moon – the start of a waning Moon period – when the accompanying reduced appetite and increased physiological efficiency work together to aid weight loss.

The dates on which the New Moon and Full Moon occur

1994	1995	1996	1997	1998	1999
Jan 11 N	Jan 01 N	Jan 05 F	Jan 09 N	Jan 12 F	Jan 02 F
Jan 27 F	Jan 16 F	Jan 20 N	Jan 23 F	Jan 28 N	Jan 17 N
Feb 10 N	Jan 30 N	Feb 04 F	Feb 07 N	Feb 11 F	Jan 31 F
Feb 26 F	Feb 15 F	Feb 18 N	Feb 22 F	Feb 26 N	Feb 16 N
Mar 12 N	Mar 01 N	Mar 05 F	Mar 09 N	Mar 13 F	Mar 02 F
Mar 27 F	Mar 17 F	Mar 19 N	Mar 24 F	Mar 28 N	Mar 17 N
Apr 11 N	Mar 31 N	Apr 04 F	Apr 07 N	Apr 11 F	Mar 31 F
Apr 25 F	Apr 15 F	Apr 17 N	Apr 22 F	Apr 26 N	Apr 16 N
May 10 N	Apr 29 N	May 03 F	May 06 N	May 11 F	Apr 30 F
May 25 F	May 14 F	May 17 N	May 22 F	May 25 N	May 15 N
Jun 09 N	May 29 N	Jun 01 F	Jun 05 N	Jun 10 F	May 30 F
Jun 23 F	Jun 13 F	Jun 16 N	Jun 20 F	Jun 24 N	Jun 13 N
Jul 08 N	Jun 28 N	Jul 01 F	Jul 04 N	Jul 09 F	Jun 28 F
Jul 22 F	Jul 12 F	Jul 15 N	Jul 20 F	Jul 23 N	Jul 13 N
Aug 07 N	Jul 27 N	Jul 30 F	Aug 03 N	Aug 08 F	Jul 28 F
Aug 21 F	Aug 10 F	Aug 14 N	Aug 18 F	Aug 22 N	Aug 11 N
Sep 05 N	Aug 26 N	Aug 28 F	Sep 01 N	Sep 06 F	Aug 26 F
Sep 19 F	Sep 09 F	Sep 12 N	Sep 16 F	Sep 20 N	Sep 09 N
Oct 05 N	Sep 24 N	Sep 27 F	Oct 01 N	Oct 05 F	Sep 25 F
Oct 19 F	Oct 08 F	Oct 12 N	Oct 16 F	Oct 20 N	Oct 09 N
Nov 03 N	Oct 24 N	Oct 26 F	Oct 31 N	Nov 04 F	Oct 24 F
Nov 18 F	Nov 07 F	Nov 11 N	Nov 14 F	Nov 19 N	Nov 08 N
Dec 02 N	Nov 22 N	Nov 25 F	Nov 30 N	Dec 03 F	Nov 23 F
Dec 18 F	Dec 07 F	Dec 10 N	Dec 14 F	Dec 18 N	Dec 07 N
	Dec 22 N	Dec 24 F	Dec 29 N		Dec 22 F

between January 1994 and the end of the millennium are given on the previous page (N = New Moon; F = Full Moon).

This information together with that given in the table on page 29, will allow you to plan exactly when is the best time to begin your diet.

3

Health Hazards and Herbal Healing

Such as are astrologers (and indeed none else are fit to make physicians) such I advise; let the planet that governs the herb be angular, and the stronger the better; if they can, in herbs of Saturn, let Saturn be in the ascendant; in the herbs of Mars, let Mars be in the Mid-heaven, for in those houses they delight; let the Moon apply to them by good aspect, and let her not be in the houses of her enemies; if you cannot well stay till she apply to them, let her apply to a planet of the same triplicity; if you cannot wait that time neither, let her be with a fixed star of their nature.

From *Culpeper's Complete Herbal*

GOOD HEALTH is not simply a blessing, it is the greatest blessing. Without it everything we do or aspire to is compromised, for the weakness and discomfort, even pain, caused by ill-health prevents our enjoyment of life and retards our progress through it. This is why a sick person is a second-class citizen where his or her ambitions and happiness are concerned.

Yet we are fortunate today, thanks to the progress of medical science, in suffering far less, if at all, from certain diseases, notably the often fatal infectious ones like the plague, smallpox, cholera, typhoid fever, typhus, and dysentery, than were people of the past. But while we are generally healthier, at least in the West, we are still susceptible to those disorders caused by the malfunction of one or other of our body parts, which can result in conditions such as arthritis, diabetes, angina pectoris, stomach ulcers, and Alzheimer's disease. We are also threatened by those we bring down upon our own heads through smoking, drinking too much, or by taking drugs. And we are, of course, all vulnerable at times to a host of minor ailments, like colds, cold sores, short sightedness, repetitive strain injuries, headaches, and allergies that cause distress and inconvenience even if they do not cripple or kill.

In fact each of us is flawed in some way, having one or more body parts particularly susceptible to disease. These are our personal weak spots. But because everyone's physical frailties and potential health complaints can be discovered through astrology, the appropriate preventative measures can be taken to stop or retard the onset of such diseases.

This knowledge is possible because each organ and part of the body is associated with or ruled by one or other of the zodiac signs. The table overleaf summarises the body parts ruled by each zodiac sign.

Your own delicate or vulnerable body areas, and thus those most liable to infection and/or health breakdown, are those ruled by your Sun sign; those ruled by the sign lying seventh from it (its opposite in your horoscope); and those ruled by your rising sign or ascendant. Indeed of the three signs, the parts governed by the last are the most susceptible to disease. This is doubly true if your Sun sign and rising sign happen to be the same.

Thus for a Virgo born at 11 a.m. GMT, the weak body areas will be those governed by Virgo (the Sun sign), Pisces (the opposite sign), and Scorpio (the rising sign). We should therefore expect this person to be most at risk from bladder, genital, and/or lower bowel disorders (due to Scorpio); intestinal and/or abdominal disorders, and nervous problems (due to Virgo); and lastly foot and/or emotional disorders (due to Pisces). Yet while all these parts are at risk, they may remain healthy due to the fact that none of the zodiac signs in question was afflicted by negative planetary influences when the person was born. Indeed, the nature of any disease, whether it be serious or not, and the specific organ or part

Zodiac sign	Body part(s) it rules
Aries:	head, brain;
Taurus:	lower jaw, ears, neck, throat, oesophagus, thyroid gland;
Gemini:	mouth, chest, collar bones, shoulder blades, windpipe, lungs, hands, arms, capillaries, nervous system;
Cancer:	stomach, breasts, ovaries, fallopian tubes, uterus, lymph glands, elbow joints;
Leo:	heart, circulatory system, upper back, spinal cord;
Virgo:	abdomen and intestines, central nervous system;
Libra:	kidneys, ureters, vagina, lower back, buttocks;
Scorpio:	bladder, lower bowel, rectum, anus, external genitalia;
Sagittarius:	hips, thighs, sciatic nerves;
Capricorn:	knees, skeleton in general, skin;
Aquarius:	lower legs and ankles;
Pisces:	feet.

likely to be affected, can only be determined from an examination of the planets in the birth chart, which is outside the scope of this book. This chapter can therefore serve only as a guide to your possible future health problems.

The commonest disorders linked with each zodiac sign are given below, along with two or more safe and effective herbal remedies that can be used in treating some of them. It will often be necessary to drink a standard brew made from the herb in question. The making of a standard brew is straightforward and is done as follows:

1) Place the herb part (flowers, leaves or roots) in a saucepan and add the required amount of fresh (preferably spring)

water. The usual ratio is one loose handful of herb material to two cups of water.

2) Heat the water slowly until it boils, then allow the herbs to simmer for about three minutes, keeping the saucepan covered.

3) Remove the saucepan from the heat, place it to one side to cool and allow the herbs to steep for twelve hours.

4) Do not strain the mixture, but put it all in a glass jar and replace the lid. The brew may be kept in a refrigerator to hinder fermentation. (If desired, you may remove the plant material after two days).

5) Spoonfuls of the liquid may now be drunk, as required. If fermentation bubbles appear in it, discard it and make a fresh standard brew.

ARIES: Aries rules the head and the brain, yet only part of the face (see below), which is why those with Aries rising or with an Aries Sun sign tend to suffer from headaches and migraine attacks, sinusitis, nasal disorders, alopecia, dandruff and other hair conditions, certain allergies, Bell's palsy, mood disorders like depression and paranoia, various psychiatric difficulties including phobias, insomnia, memory loss, and chronic degenerative conditions of the brain, such as Alzheimer's disease. The eyes may also be afflicted in some way, e.g. short sight or cataracts. Arians are similarly prone to head injuries brought about by their involvement in sports and other hazardous activities, and by their impulsiveness. They can of course prevent or moderate such injuries by wearing the right safety equipment and by concentrating on what they are doing. Because Libra is the seventh sign from Aries, the Aries-born suffer secondarily from the weaknesses and disorders outlined below for Libra.

One good remedy for headaches is to apply cold mint tea to the forehead. Its effectiveness is increased by steeping slices of fresh potato in the mint tea for one hour, after which they should be laid on the forehead and held in place by a cloth dampened with the tea. A standard brew of mint tea is made by using the leaves and stems of ordinary garden mint (*Mentha viridis*). The brew can also be drunk warm or cold to improve the memory and to prevent indigestion. Mint is ruled by Venus, who in myth was the lover and calmer of the warlike Mars.

Another Venus-ruled herb that is effective against headaches is the cowslip (*Primula veris*). Because only the flowers of this spring herb are used, they should be picked in May or June, when it is in full bloom and most potent, then dried and stored for later use. Make a standard brew, adding honey as a sweetener if required, and drink a cupful to remedy a headache or before retiring to bed to prevent insomnia. Cowslip tea has a generally calming effect on the mind and is thus very beneficial for those ruled by Aries.

The parts of the face governed by the zodiac signs are as follows:

Aries:	right nostril
Taurus:	middle of forehead, left ear
Gemini:	mouth
Cancer:	left eye, upper part of forehead
Leo:	right eye, lower forehead
Virgo:	right cheek
Libra:	left nostril, right ear
Scorpio:	nose
Sagittarius:	right eyebrow
Capricorn:	chin
Aquarius:	left eyebrow
Pisces:	left cheek

TAURUS: Taurus rules the neck, which includes each of its separate parts, namely the throat, epiglottis and oesophagus, the larynx, the neck muscles, the tonsils, the adenoids, the thyroid gland, and the cervical vertebrae (but not the trachea or windpipe), and the lower jaw and the left ear. Hence those with the Sun in Taurus or with Taurus rising are particularly susceptible to sore throats, laryngitis, tonsillitis and other throat infections, polyps, catarrh, voice loss, speech defects, goitre and related thyroid gland abnormalities, throat tumours, both malignant and benign, neck injuries, earache and hearing difficulties. Such conditions may also be suffered by those born under Scorpio, the seventh sign from Taurus in the zodiac. Taurus individuals are likewise secondarily susceptible to those weaknesses and disorders described for Scorpio.

One of the best remedies for sore throats involves the leaves of the common violet (*Viola odorata*), which is ruled by Venus and so is ideal for the task. The leaves can either be used fresh or can be dried for later use. Make a standard brew with them and gargle with the liquid as required. Damp leaves from the brew can be applied as a healing poultice to mouth and other ulcers.

Another excellent herbal cure for throat conditions is the aptly named Throatwort or Canterbury Bell (*Campanula trachelium*). Make a standard brew with the leaves. Use it as a gargle or drink it as a tea. It is particularly effective against mouth ulcers.

Lastly, another mouth and throat soother is ginger (*Zingiber spp.*). Either chew a small piece of the root or drink a cupful of ginger tea, made by stirring a quarter of a teaspoon of powdered ginger into half a pint of hot water. Ginger thus taken also has the ability to correct delayed menstruation, which makes it particularly helpful to Taurean (or Scorpio) women who might be so afflicted.

GEMINI: The lips and the mouth, also the chest and its contents (notably the trachea and the lungs, but not the heart), are ruled by Gemini, as are the shoulders, the arms and the hands. The sign shares the rulership of the ribs with Cancer, Gemini being the lord of the upper ribs, Cancer of the lower ribs. The nervous system is also partly ruled by Gemini. Those born under it are likely to suffer from muscle and joint injuries of these parts, and/or from conditions such as rheumatism and arthritis affecting them. They are most at risk, however, from lung ailments, which means that coughs, asthma, pneumonia, emphysema, bronchitis, lung cancer and related diseases are common among them. This is why Geminis, in order to protect their lungs, should not smoke tobacco or work in dusty, air-polluted environments. They also have a highly strung nervous system, which is particularly susceptible to stress. Many Geminis are over-anxious and fidgety, and hence find it hard to relax. They are also prone to mouth ulcers, cold sores and other mouth or lip conditions, to which their over-anxiety contributes. Because Sagittarius is the seventh sign from Gemini, the Gemini-born are secondarily susceptible to those weaknesses and disorders described for Sagittarians.

The root of the liquorice (*Glycyrrhiza glabra*) is an old specific for both throat and lung complaints, including coughs, pleurisy and bronchitis. When available, the raw root should be chewed to obtain relief, although liquorice eaten in the form of sweets or liquorice sticks is also effective.

The flowers and/or the leaves of the honeysuckle (*Lonicera caprifolium*), a plant ruled by Mercury, can be used to make a standard brew that is efficacious in treating asthma and other respiratory problems. Drink a cupful before retiring at night, or when needed, to relieve the chest ailment. Honeysuckle thus taken is also useful in treating disorders of the spleen.

Gemini anxiety can be lessened by regularly eating the finely chopped leaves and flowers of rosemary (*Rosmarinus officinalis*) added to soups and salads, while a sudden upsurge of worry may be dealt with by drinking a tablespoonful of the standard brew. Thus ingested rosemary is also said to improve the memory and soothe the stomach. Indeed, this herb is one of the best nerve and digestive tonics. Because of its calming effect, rosemary will also help combat sleeplessness, as will eating a tablespoonful of honey at dinnertime.

CANCER: Cancer governs the stomach in both sexes and thus the digestion that takes place within it. It also rules the breasts and the female internal reproductive parts, namely the ovaries, the uterus, and the fallopian tubes, but not the vagina. It also rules over the lower ribs, the sternum and the diaphragm. Those both with the Sun in Cancer or with Cancer rising tend to be particularly susceptible to stomach problems, like indigestion, dyspepsia, stomach ulcers, and cramps and stomach pains, and it takes little to make them vomit. The breasts and the internal reproductive parts are also weak spots in the female Cancer's body. This is why she often suffers from menstrual cramps and related disorders, and why she should routinely examine her breasts and have regular gynaecological check-ups. Any form of emotional upset is hard for Cancerians of either sex to cope with or to bear, especially as they are born worriers, which explains why they can only function properly and feel happy in a secure and loving environment. Hence it is hardly surprising that they are prone to emotionally-based eating disorders, like anorexia nervosa and bulimia. Cancerians are secondarily vulnerable to those ailments described for Capricorn, the seventh sign from Cancer, just as Capricorns are likely to suffer from those affecting Cancer.

One of the most beneficial herbs for digestive disorders is dill (*Anethum graveolens*), a commonly grown, Mercury-ruled garden plant. The leaves may be eaten raw or can be used to make a standard brew, two tablespoons of which should be swallowed before meals. Thus taken, dill soothes the stomach and aids digestion, and helps to prevent flatulence. It also calms the emotions and has a beneficial effect on both hair and nail growth.

The Moon-ruled cabbage plant (*Brassica oleracea*) is also very useful in treating both digestive complaints and gastric ulcers. The leaves may be eaten in the normal way as a vegetable, although they are more efficacious when they are juiced and a cupful of the liquid drunk morning and night. If you prefer, make and eat a traditional French cabbage soup. This will add good gastronomic pleasure to herbal thaumaturgy.

LEO: Because Leo rules the heart and the circulatory system, these are especially vulnerable to disease in those born under Leo or who have Leo rising. Heart conditions include angina pectoris, pericarditis, endocarditis, and coronary thrombosis. Embolism and arteriosclerosis are two disorders that may affect the blood vessels. This is why Leos or those with Leo rising should not place themselves at further risk by smoking, drinking heavily, or by eating fatty foods. Stress should also be avoided. Bruising, broken veins, and varicose veins are also common to those born under Leo. The sign additionally rules the upper back, which includes the rib (or thoracic) region of the spine and the spinal cord, and some astrologers also claim that it has governance over the radius and ulna bones of the forearm. Hence injuries to and disorders of these parts are quite common among those governed by Leo. This is also true of eye disorders, as Leo is given rulership of the right eye, the latter being particularly vulnerable to infection and injury. These body parts are also at risk for those born under Aquarius, which is the seventh sign from Leo in the zodiac, in the same way that Leos are secondarily vulnerable to the diseases and injuries described for Aquarius.

One of the best herbs to eat for maintaining the health of the heart is watercress (*Nasturtium officinale*), which can be readily and cheaply obtained in season and which should be eaten raw in large quantities as often as possible. If preferred, watercress can be drunk by being finely chopped and stirred into cold skimmed milk. Its high iron content is the reason why the herb is put under the rulership of Mars and why it is a specific against anaemia. This explains why watercress is said to restore the colour to the cheeks. It additionally elevates the mood.

The appearance of broken blood vessels in the skin can be remedied by the eating of chives (*Allium schoenoprasum*). These are most pleasantly and conveniently ingested when chopped and added as a seasoning to vegetables like carrots and potatoes, or to salads, soups, omelettes and other dishes.

VIRGO: The sign of Virgo is given dominion over the abdomen and the organs it contains, most notably the small and large intestines, and the solar plexus. It also shares governance of the nervous system with Gemini. In the face it rules the right cheek. Those with a Virgo Sun sign or who have Virgo rising, tend to be rather nervous, highly strung people who are vulnerable to stress, and whose inner tensions and anxieties prompt the digestive upsets and abdominal aches and pains that so commonly afflict them. They are particularly at risk from duodenal ulcers, spastic colon, diverticulitis, appendicitis, bowel disorders, including constipation, and flatulence. This is why the Virgo-born should not only pay attention to their diet, but should practise meditation and other mind-calming techniques to help allay their inherent anxiety. They should avoid stress. They are secondarily susceptible to those disorders described for Pisceans, the seventh sign from Virgo in the zodiac, who in turn may also suffer from those disorders characteristic of Virgoans.

Fennel (*Foeniculum vulgare*), ruled by Mercury, is one of the best herbal remedies for flatulence. The leaves of the plant may either be eaten raw or, more pleasantly, in a sauce to accompany fish. The leaves are also said to calm the nerves, prevent constipation (as will fennel roots), and generally clear up intestinal disorders. In ancient Rome gladiators ate fennel to give them courage.

The aptly named All-Heal or valerian (*Valeriana officinalis*) is also ruled by Mercury, which is why it is excellent for treating Virgoan nervous disorders. The plant was once used to treat epilepsy by the American Indians. Make a standard brew with the thinly sliced roots, and take two tablespoonfuls of it three times a day to combat anxiety and other nervous disorders. Be warned, however, that its taste and odour are rather unpleasant.

LIBRA: Libra rules the lower back including the lumbar region of the spine, the kidneys and ureters, the vagina, and the buttocks. Back injuries like slipped discs and pulled muscles are prevalent among those born under Libra or who have Libra rising. They should therefore be particularly careful when bending or when lifting anything. The Libran-born are also susceptible to disorders affecting the kidneys, such as nephritis, Bright's disease, kidney stones, and renal failure. Because the kidneys remove wastes from the body as urine, the Libra person should certainly avoid drug-taking or drinking too much alcohol, which can damage them. Libra women are prone to developing thrush, herpes, and other vaginal disorders. Those born under Aries, the seventh zodiac sign from Libra, are similarly susceptible to these diseases, in the same way that migraines and other Aries head complaints affect Libras.

The dandelion (*Taraxacum officinale*) is a common weed but one of the most useful and nutritious of plants. Ruled by Jupiter (although some astrologers say by the Sun), its flowers can be made into wine, its leaves eaten as a salad vegetable, and its roots ground to make a healthy coffee-like drink. While all are beneficial for treating kidney disorders, the best effects are gained by either eating a handful of the raw leaves daily or by drinking three tablespoonfuls twice a day of a standard brew made with them. This will promote the flow of urine and generally tone up the kidneys, help prevent obesity, combat over-tiredness, benefit the liver and relieve the symptoms of rheumatoid arthritis. The dandelion is also helpful to the heart.

The Venus-ruled strawberry (*Fragaria vesca*) is likewise a good diuretic, as well as being effective for dissolving tartar on the teeth and uplifting the spirits. Eat the ripe red fruits to obtain these benefits. Should gravel be present in either the kidneys or the bladder, or both, it can be remedied by drinking a standard brew made with strawberry leaves.

Kidney and bladder stones can also be remedied by eating a handful of raw asparagus shoots (*Asparagus officinalis*) before meals.

SCORPIO: The sign of the Scorpion has rulership over the external genitalia, the bladder and urethra, the rectum and anus, and the prostate gland. Those born with the Sun in Scorpio or with Scorpio rising tend to suffer from diseases of these parts, which can range from the commonly occurring lower bowel disorders of constipation and haemorrhoids to bowel cancer; bed wetting, urinary leakage, and other bladder complaints; prostate problems; sexual difficulties including impotence and sterility; ruptures; and venereal infections, including AIDS, which can result from the promiscuous behaviour of many Scorpios. Their lower bowel sensitivity makes it particularly important for Scorpios to eat a high fibre diet, while their often irresponsible sexual behaviour should be modified to avoid either contracting or passing on a venereal infection. They would be wise not to let embarrassment prevent them from consulting a doctor should they fear they have some disorder or disease of the body parts in question. Scorpios are likewise secondarily vulnerable to the disorders described for Taurus, the seventh sign of the zodiac from Scorpio, in the same way that the Taurus-born are susceptible to the disedases or health problems affecting Scorpios.

The fruits or leaves of the strawberry can be eaten, as described above, to treat gravel and other bladder conditions. Strawberries also have a beneficial effect upon the stomach, the liver, and the bowels.

Another highly beneficial, remedial plant is the stinging nettle (*Urtica dioica*), which is ruled, perhaps not surprisingly, by Mars. The young leaves and shoots can be made into a vitamin and iron-rich standard brew, and the resulting liquid can be used externally as an effective hair rinse and conditioner, or drunk to cure anaemia, asthma, infertility, gout, obesity, rheumatism, and sciatica. Used as a gargle it will soothe soreness of the mouth and throat. Nettle tea and nettle beer are still made and enjoyed in some country districts, with the same beneficial results.

SAGITTARIUS: Sagittarius rules over the hips and the hip joints, the thighs or upper legs, and the liver, so these parts are the medically weak spots for those born with the Sun in Sagittarius or with Sagittarius rising. They often suffer from hip problems of one sort or another, particularly arthritis and other conditions affecting the hip joints, from sciatica, and from liver conditions brought on by their often immoderate eating and drinking habits. They are similarly susceptible to gout. Hip and thigh injuries are commonly sustained during the rough body-contact sports that they love to play. Sagittarius is the seventh zodiac sign from Gemini so Sagittarians are susceptible to the negative pulmonary and other health conditions described for Gemini.

The herb comfrey (*Symphytum officinalis*) is ideal for the treatment of Sagittarian injuries – its country name is Knit-Bone – and for several other health problems affecting the sign. Indeed, sprains, bruises, and swellings, including those caused by insect bites and stings, can effectively be treated by applying a poultice of comfrey leaves and bandaging them in place. Rub the leaves gently on the skin to relieve any itching or irritation. For speeding the healing of fractures, restoring torn ligaments, easing the discomfort of rheumatism and arthritis, and alleviating bronchial and other pulmonary complaints, either eat three or four fresh comfrey leaves each day or make a standard brew with them and drink a cupful before meals.

The chervil (*Anthriscus cerefolium*) is commonly cultivated in gardens, although it also grows wild in hedgerows. The fresh leaves can be grated into soups, sauces, omelettes, etc. Ruled by Jupiter, the chervil is most useful as a general tonic, as it lifts the spirits and helps to restore the memory. The leaves may be dried and made into a tea or used fresh to make a standard brew, a wine glassful of which should be drunk in the morning and in the evening.

CAPRICORN: The sign of the Goat is given rulership over not only the patellae or knee caps and the knee-joints, but the skin (which includes the hair and the nails), and the skeleton in general, including the teeth. This is why those born with the Sun in Capricorn or with Capricorn rising suffer more than most from ailments affecting the knees, such as house-maid's knee, arthritis of the knees (and other joints), and dislocations of the patella and other knee injuries; from skin, hair and nail problems, like acne, impetigo, warts, broken nails, dandruff, eczema, shingles, psoriasis and, at worst, cancer; and from various bone and teeth disorders. It is therefore most important that Capricorns eat a good, wholesome diet, particularly one rich in milk products, fruits and vegetables, which will supply them with all the vitamins and minerals (especially calcium) they need to make strong bones, sound teeth, and a healthy skin. (Capricorns unfortunately have a tendency to favour odd assortments of scraps.) Cancer is the seventh sign of the zodiac from Capricorn, which means that the negative health conditions described for it are also likely to afflict the Capricorn born.

The houseleek (*Sempervivum tectorum*) is a perennial herb whose succulent leaves provide one of the best remedies for dermal itching and warts. Where the latter are concerned, simply slice one of the leaves in two and press the moist surface to the wart. Itching can be relieved by pulping the leaves and applying the mash to the afflicted part.

Skin problems, including itching, can be countered by the daisy (*Bellis perennis*), although this Venus-ruled plant is, as the Latin name suggests, primarily a wound herb. Make a standard brew using the leaves, and drink two tablespoonfuls three times a day to clear the complexion and cure skin infections. Both skin wounds and bruises can be relieved by moistening a pad with the brew, then applying it directly to them and bandaging it in place.

AQUARIUS: The Water Pourer has governance over the lower legs and the ankles, which naturally includes the tibia and fibula bones, and their muscles and other tissues. It is for this reason that those born under Aquarius or who have Aquarius rising are vulnerable to injuries and disorders of these parts. They are particularly likely to sprain or otherwise damage their ankles, which suggests they should avoid activities, like jumping, that put an undue strain on them or twist them. Knee injuries are also quite common among Aquarians, for although Capricorn rules the knees, the tibia forms part of the knee joint. Calf muscle cramps and varicose veins are two other conditions that also frequently affect Aquarians. It is therefore important for them to avoid long periods of sitting down, and to take a brisk walk every day. The seventh zodiac sign from Aquarius is Leo so Aquarians share the Leo's negative heart and circulatory susceptibilities.

Perhaps the best and most easily obtained remedy for varicose veins is provided by the Mars-ruled sheep's parsley or wild carrot (*Daucus carota*) and its garden varieties. The treatment consists of making a standard brew with the flowers of the carrot plant (wild or domestic), and a glassful of the liquid should be drunk before each meal. One or more raw carrots may be eaten to obtain similar, although slightly less effective relief. Carrots also work well against stomach ulcers, liver complaints, kidney and bladder disorders, menstrual pain, diabetes, and reputedly cancer.

Garden peas (*Pisum sativum*) are efficacious in reducing the size and tempering the pain of varicose veins and haemorrhoids. Peas are also said to 'sweeten' the blood. The peas used should be freshly shelled, not the tinned variety, and cooked in the normal way. Ideally they are eaten as an accompaniment to boiled or mashed potatoes and fowl.

PISCES: The feet are ruled by Pisces, which is why those born under the sign or who have Pisces rising are susceptible to foot problems of one sort or another. These include injuries to the feet; growth abnormalities like ingrowing toe-nails and hammer toes; foot ulcers, corns and verrucas; cold feet and other circulation-related disorders like chilblains and frostbite; and infectious diseases such as athlete's foot. The natural emotional sensitivity of Pisceans makes them susceptible to the effects of stress, which may in turn prompt them to drink excessively or to take drugs. Because their opposite sign is Virgo, they may suffer from many of the afflictions that plague those born under this sign, such as indigestion, constipation, and flatulence.

An excellent herbal remedy for Piscean chilblains is a lotion made from the bulbs of the Moon-ruled snowdrop (*Galanthus nivalis*). Take four bulbs of the plant, slice them finely and steep the slices overnight in half a pint of beer. Apply the resulting lotion to the affected part in the morning and at night or when needed to relieve discomfort. If the feet are frostbitten, add one heaped teaspoonful of cayenne pepper to the lotion and apply as before.

Those suffering from constipation, lack of appetite, indigestion, or even headaches, can obtain relief by eating the red leaf stems or 'sticks' of rhubarb (*Rheum rhaponticum*). If possible, eat them raw, otherwise consume in the normal way by making them into a dessert. Rhubarb is particularly effective in treating bowel irregularity when it is combined and eaten with the leaves of senna (*Cassia acutifolia*). This combination is guaranteed to loosen even the most recalcitrant bowels!

In recent times, tree-hugging, that is, the embracing of tree trunks, has become popular among those who regard themselves as 'green'. While a laudable activity that brings people and trees into close and, it is hoped, comforting proximity, tree hugging's mutual effectiveness is often diminished, if not completely negated, by the astrological incompatibility of human being and tree. For each tree, like ourselves, is governed by one of the planets, and when a tree is to be tightly clasped by someone whose astrological type is quite different from its own it is both distasteful and distressing to it. Yet when compatibility exists, the tree will not only be reassured by such a display of affection but will possibly allow its spiritual self to enter into a deeper and more meaningful contact with that of the person. In a similar manner, the nuts of some trees are particularly compatible with the physical make up of those who share the tree's planetary ruler.

Below are the planetary rulers of the commonest trees, which will enable tree huggers and nut eaters to gain the best rapport with these lofty and beneficial plants. Hug the trunks and eat the nuts of those trees whose ruler is the same as that of your Sun sign or of your rising sign.

The Sun (Leo) rules:	ash, bay, birch, juniper, laurel, vine, walnut;
The Moon (Cancer) rules:	white poplar, willow;
Mercury (Gemini, Virgo) rules:	almond, hazel, liquorice, mulberry, myrtle;
Venus (Taurus, Libra) rules:	alder (black and common), cherry,

	elder, peach, pear, plum, sweet chestnut, sycamore;
Mars (Aries, Scorpio) rules:	box, hawthorn, holly, pine;
Jupiter (Sagittarius, Pisces) rules:	fig, horse chestnut, lime-tree or linden, maple, oak, spruce;
Saturn (Capricorn, Aquarius) rules:	beech, black poplar, black willow, cornel, cypress, elm, gall-oak, quince, rowan, sloe, yew

Tree huggers might like to remember that several tree species were originally women or nymphs, at least according to the ancient Greeks. Some of these women were changed into trees to protect them from being ravished, while others were transformed while grieving for a loved one. All might appreciated some sympathy.

The nymph Daphne, for example, was changed into a laurel tree to escape the amorous attentions of the god Apollo, and the nymph Pitys was turned into a pine tree to elude the god Pan. The almond tree, however, was formed from Phyllis, who died of grief when her lover Acamas failed to return from the Trojan War. The white poplar, or alder, was created from the two divine sisters Prote and Clymene, daughters of the Sun, who were killed by Zeus along with their brother Phaethon, when the boy drove his father's chariot foolishly and careeringly across the sky.

4

Looking Good, Feeling Great

Exercise cannot secure us from that dissolution to which we are decreed; but while the soul and body continue united, it can make the association pleasing, and give probable hopes that they shall be disjoined by an easy separation.

From *The Rambler No. 85* by Samuel Johnson

I T GOES without saying that we all want to look as attractive as possible and to feel fit and well. The two states usually, of course, go together. An unfit person is typically tired and lethargic, and looks that way too, whereas someone who is fit not only has more energy and zest for life, but is lit up from within by them, which enhances his or her attractiveness.

Wellness is not simply the absence of disease, but is rather the product of a number of factors, which include, along with a freedom from illness, good nutrition, adequate sleep, manageable stress, and sufficient exercise. With all these, you are blessed indeed and you will look your best, with sparkling eyes, glowing skin, a readiness to smile, and an upright, confident stance. Without them your appearance will suffer.

If you have begun to put into practice the astrological dietary advice given in Chapter Two, then you will no doubt have started to feel some benefit. Your taste-buds should be satisfied, your bowel movements will have become regular, and your body will be better nourished. Most importantly, from a psychological point of view, you will have started to shed any excess pounds so that you look trimmer. This is why a good diet is one of the keys to making the most of yourself.

Restful Nights

A good diet will also help you to sleep better, as sound sleep is prompted by dietary harmony. Yet sleeplessness or broken sleep is often caused by worry, which is why insomnia commonly affects the more anxious Sun sign types, namely Geminis, Cancers, Virgos, Libras, Scorpios, and Pisceans, or those who have one of these signs rising. Poor sleep not only negatively affects our looks, but makes us bad tempered and irritable.

If you have an anxious nature it is very hard, if not impossible, to stop worrying completely. And because a bad sleep pattern tends to create the expectation that we will sleep badly, sleeplessness often continues even when the original worry has been dealt with.

There are, however, some effective and harmless aids to good sleep, which you might like to try. They are based on the astrological associations of the Moon, the ruler of the night.

Good sleep, for example, is encouraged by wearing to bed a ring, bracelet or necklace made of silver, which is the metal of the Moon. Its potency in this regard is increased if the item bears one or more of the Moon's gemstones, which are moonstone, turquoise, quartz, and pearl. Ideally these should touch the skin, which they will if they form part of an open backed ring or are worn as a pendant. A piece of coral either worn or placed near your bed will have the same effect. Another stone that encourages sleep if placed beside the bed is the magnetic lodestone, although this is ruled by Mars, not the Moon.

Two completely safe sleep enhancers are lettuce and milk, both of which are Moon-ruled. If you eat two or three lettuce leaves or drink some warm milk before you retire you will soon drift off to the land of Nod. Indeed, there is no reason why you shouldn't wash down the lettuce leaves with the milk to be doubly sure.

Lettuce tea can be made by boiling some lettuce leaves in water. If you drink a cupful before retiring it will not only bring you pleasant dreams, but will also stimulate your bowels during the night and reduce your sex urge.

If you prefer, you can simmer a couple of lettuce leaves for three minutes in half a pint of water to which a few drops of oil of roses have been added. Strain the solution when it has cooled, and then, before you lie down for the night, gently rub some of it on your forehead with cotton wool. Once dry, it will help you to both sleep well and have pleasant dreams.

Lastly, good sleep can be had by eating a spoonful of honey, whose sleep-inducing properties derive from the Moon-ruled nectar gathered by bees, before you to to bed.

People who normally sleep well often find that their sleep is disturbed at Full Moon. If you are one of these, you should find that one of the methods described above can prevent such occasional lunar restlessness.

Improving Your Looks

It is always a good idea to take into account the phases of the Moon when scheduling any activity undertaken to improve your appearance, whether this be visiting your hairdresser, buying make-up or clothes, or having a manicure or pedicure. In general, such improvements work most successfully if they are carried out when the Moon is waxing, or changing from New to Full. The waning Moon, by contrast, tends to curtail or spoil any efforts made, unless your object is some sort of re-duction, such as losing weight.

For example, if you wish to thicken or speed up the growth of your hair, always have it cut when the Moon is waxing. Or try washing it with milk, which again is best done when the Moon is waxing. But if you want to slow down the growth of unwanted body hair, then shave it or use a depilatory cream when the Moon is waning.

You should, of course, wash your hair regularly, using the right shampoo for your hair type. If you suffer from dandruff use a medicated shampoo until the condition has been elim-inated. Then simply use the same shampoo from time to time to stop the dandruff coming back.

You can easily make an excellent hair beautifier from Mars-ruled stinging nettles. Take about one handful of dried nettle leaves, simmer them in one quart of water for two hours, allow the liquid to cool, and then strain it into a bottle. If you rub some of the liquid into your scalp every night it will fight dandruff, strengthen your hair, improve its growth, and give it an attractive sheen. It is also said to prevent baldness in men. The appearance of your hair can be further enhanced by rubbing a few drops of rosemary oil into it, which will also give it a sweet smell. Nettles can be dried by either hanging a few stems up, or by spreading the leaves on trays, in a warm place like a kitchen. But be warned that dry nettles may still sting, so always handle them with caution.

Lettuce, cucumber, and watercress are all ruled by the Moon, which is why they, along with onions and lemons, are traditionally used, either alone or in lotions, to improve the complexion. If you have any problems with your skin, you might like to try one or other of the following skin improvement methods.

Slices of cucumber can be used to freshen and soften your complexion. First wash and dry your face. Cut several thin slices of cucumber, then lie on your back and spread the slices over your face. Now relax for 20 minutes to half an hour in order to give the cucumber time to work its magic. You can also place cold moist tea bags on your eyes at the same time to help reduce any puffiness around them or darkness under them.

To make a good face-pack, juice half a medium sized cucumber in a blender, add a few drops of fresh lemon juice and then beat in the white of an egg. Apply the resulting mixture to your face, allow it to dry, then wash it off with cold water. This lunar face-pack will help banish wrinkles, fade freckles, and generally improve the complexion. Use it at least once a week, preferably on a Monday.

Another excellent face-pack can be made by beating together one egg-white, a teaspoonful of olive oil and one tablespoon of clear honey. That done, cover the mixing bowl with a damp cloth and put it to one side. Steam your face over a bowl of boiling water to which chopped fresh herbs like mint, rosemary and thyme have been added. Cover your head with a towel to concentrate the steam on your face. Do this for about ten minutes. The steam will open your pores and help remove impurities from your skin. Now dab your face dry with a clean towel and, using some cotton wool, apply a mild skin tonic. Next spread the face-pack over your face. Leave it on until it is dry, then wash it off with lukewarm water. Do not put anything else on your face before retiring to bed for the night. This steam/face-pack complexion improver is of course most effective if used when the Moon is waxing.

If your skin is greasy you will find it helpful to dab your whole face with freshly squeezed lemon juice. Let the juice dry on your skin, then go to bed. The lemon odour will also help you to sleep. An excellent lemon skin lotion can be made by mixing together one ounce of fresh, strained lemon juice with three ounces of rose water and one ounce of glycerine. Rub this into your face and hands daily. Again, make the lotion when the Moon is waxing.

Spots and pimples can be dealt with by crushing onions in vinegar (co-ruled by the Moon and the Sun) and applying the mixture to them. Leave it on for about ten minutes, then wash it off. However, because the mixture is somewhat strong-smelling it is best applied (and removed!) before you go to bed. Remember that as spots and pimples are skin blemishes, their elimination is most readily achieved during a waning Moon.

Keeping Regular

If you normally evacuate your bowels once a day, such regularity will help to keep your skin clear and fresh. Skin problems, however, are aggravated by constipation, so it is in your own interest to eat a diet that will help keep you regular. Wholemeal bread, fibre-rich cereals, porridge and muesli, and fresh fruit and vegetables, can all do this. Bread and cereals also have the advantage of supplying plenty of the B vitamins, while fruit and vegetables provide lots of vitamin C, both of which are need to maintain the health of the skin and hair. Vitamin C is vital in this regard as it forms part of collagen, the protein that gives the skin its elasticity. Too little vitamin C in the diet results in thinner skin, broken veins and easy bruising, and encourages the development of wrinkles. An adequate intake of vitamin C will also help prevent that blight of teenage life, acne.

Solar Dangers

It is not a good idea to spend too long lying in the sun as its rays dry the skin and adversely affect its quality. This is why compulsive sunbathers often develop leathery and wrinkled skin, which looks unattractive and which prematurely ages them. They are also more likely to develop skin cancer. So if you want your face to be soft and unlined, stay out of the sun as much as possible. Strong sunlight also makes you wrinkle up your eyes, which encourages the development of permanent facial creases.

Unattractive facial lines are also more likely to form if you are worried or angry, as these negative emotional states produce habitual grimaces such as frowns that often become etched into the face as creases. A face always looks most beautiful when it is relaxed and composed, so you will do yourself a favour by developing a calm inner state, or at least by paying attention to your expressions and trying to moderate those that are the most distorting and damaging to your appearance.

The Best Time To Buy

Apart from using the phases of the Moon to augment the efficacy of the beauty improvement methods you use, you will also find it advantageous to exploit the position of the Moon in the zodiac. In this respect the Moon is like the Sun, travelling from one zodiac sign to the next, although because it moves far more quickly than the Sun, it passes through the entire zodiac in just under 28 days (the sidereal month) spending about two and a half days in each sign as it does so. The Moon's influence changes somewhat as it moves from sign to sign, favouring certain activities while in one sign, others when in another. This is particularly applicable to purchases of personal items. The table below shows you the best time to buy different types of clothes, make-up and similar beauty products, and other accessories. It will help you to find bargains, the right colours and sizes, and the most suitable styles.

Moon in Aries: buy after-shave, earrings, eye-shadow, face-cream, hairnets, hairsprays, hats, lipstick, razors, shaving cream, shampoo, spectacles, sun-glasses, wigs.

Moon in Taurus: buy cravats, necklaces, perfume, scarves, ties, gargles.

Moon in Gemini: buy bracelets, breath fresheners, gloves, handbags, nail polish, purses, rings, shoulder bags, wraps.

Moon in Cancer: buy bathing suits, brassieres, blouses, shirts, silver jewellery, vests.

Moon in Leo: buy brooches, clasps, coats, gold jewellery, jackets, waistcoats.

Moon in Virgo: buy aprons, belts, cummerbunds.

Moon in Libra: buy ball gowns, costumes, dresses, suits, suspender belts.

Moon in Scorpio: buy condoms, panties, slips, tampons, underpants.

Moon in Sagittarius: buy pantihose, riding and sports clothes, skirts, stockings, tights, trousers.

Moon in Capricorn: buy furs, body oils and rubs, knee supports, leather goods, suntan lotions, toothpaste, talcum powder.

Moon in Aquarius: buy pop socks, ankle chains, boots,

jodhpurs, silk stockings.

Moon in Pisces: buy foot sprays, nail polish, sandals, shoes, slippers, socks.

However, because the Moon travels so rapidly through the zodiac, lack of space prevents me from recording the future dates when it passes through each of the various signs. This information can be obtained from either an ephemeris or an almanac, both of which can be bought from most New Age bookshops and are well worth their modest cost.

Healthy Exercise

You can improve both your fitness and your looks by exercising regularly. Indeed, exercise is so important that you will never be at your best unless you do some, preferably outside in the sunlight and fresh air, but always check with your doctor before committing yourself to a programme of exercise. Yet because exercise is equated in many people's mind with jogging, lifting weights, or cavorting in leotards, they are put off by the seeming difficulty and sweaty unattractiveness of it, not to mention the expense.

Fortunately adequate and appearance-enhancing exercise can be done with a minimum of effort and at a modest cost, by following a regular work-out schedule that is in synchronisation with planetary influences. You can jog if you particularly want to, but equally good aerobic exercise can be had by cycling, swimming or walking briskly. Studies of tribes that have had no contact with modern industrial society show that they run only when chasing a hunted animal or when escaping from an enemy or predator. These people have pulse rates, blood pressure and cholesterol levels which are healthily low and probably similar to those of our primitive ancestors.

Just as the foods we eat, liquids we drink, and remedial herbs we gather, are all associated with or ruled by one or other of the seven traditional planets, so too are the days of the week. The planetary rulers of Saturday, Sunday and

Monday can be quite easily discovered in their names. Saturday is Saturn's day; Sunday is the Sun's day; and Monday is the Moon's day. The planetary rulers of the remaining four days are less easy to discern because their names derive from those of ancient and largely forgotten Scandinavian deities. Tuesday, for example is Tiw's day, Tiw being a war god, the equivalent of Mars. Wednesday is Woden's day, and Woden is equated with Mercury. Thursday is Thor's day, who is the Scandinavian Jupiter, and Friday is Frija's day, she being a love goddess like Venus. The planetary rulers of each day of the week are therefore:

Day:	Ruler:
Sunday	the Sun
Monday	the Moon
Tuesday	Mars
Wednesday	Mercury
Thursday	Jupiter
Friday	Venus
Saturday	Saturn

Such rulerships impart a particular quality to the days of the week, and make them fortunate for certain activities but less so for others. It is lucky, for example, to go sailing or fishing on a Monday because the Moon rules the sea and everything to do with it. Business activities are favoured on a Wednesday because Mercury governs, among other things, money and marketing, which is why we call those who sell 'merchants' and their goods 'merchandise'. Yet it would tempt providence to go to war on a Friday, the day of Venus, or try to paint a picture on a Tuesday, the day of Mars. Both activities are inappropriate for the day in question and would not normally be blessed by good fortune.

The exercises recommended in the following Zodiac Workout Schedule, which are each chosen for the right astrological day of the week, will help you to improve your overall fitness by shaping up your heart and lungs, strengthening and tightening your muscles, improving your muscle tone, and burning off unwanted fat. Wear something light and comfortable, such as shorts, a T-shirt and running shoes, and begin the exercises gradually. As time goes by you will be able to do more sets and more repetitions. Work through each day's exercises at whatever time is convenient for you, but don't include exercises that are astrologically wrong for the day. By putting your body in harmony with the planets and stars, you will soon look trimmer and feel much better.

Always remember to do some simple warm up exercises such as gentle running on the spot, knee bends or arm raises before embarking on the main exercise.

SUNDAY: The Sun is the ruler of Sunday and of the sign Leo, whose principal body parts are the heart, the circulatory system, and the upper back. These must therefore be exercised today.

The heart is the body's most important organ. It pumps the blood around the body through the blood vessels, thereby bringing nourishment and oxygen to all parts of it and removing carbon dioxide and other wastes. The blood also transports hormones like adrenalin, fights infection, and when necessary clots to prevent its own loss. When the heart stops beating we die.

You can improve the fitness of your heart by making it beat faster, so Sunday is the day on which you should do some aerobic exercise. Take a brisk walk of 20 to 30 minutes duration, or go cycling, swimming, or jogging. These activities also make you breathe more deeply, so benefiting your lungs, and improve your blood circulation. They all also exercise several muscle groups, including those of the upper back, for which swimming is particularly good.

One exercise for strengthening and toning the upper back muscles is as follows: Stand up straight with your feet about 24 inches apart. Then bend forward from the hips, keeping your back straight, until your upper body is parallel to the ground. Let your arms hang down, then raise them straight out from your sides as high as you can. Lower your arms and repeat five more times. This constitutes one set. Do more sets if you can.

Later, you can increase the work load by holding a book or some other weight in each hand. You can also raise your arms forward until they come up to the sides of your head.

As the Sun, like the Moon, rules only one zodiac sign, you can increase your work-out today, if you wish, by doing those exercises given for the other two signs of the Fire triplicity, namely Aries (see Tuesday) and Sagittarius (see Thursday). This will not disturb the astrological harmony of your schedule.

MONDAY: The Moon, the ruler of Monday, governs the upper abdominal muscles and the muscles underlying the breasts, therefore these are the muscles that need to be exercised today. Because the Moon rules also water and the zodiac sign Cancer, Monday is a particularly good and harmonious day on which to enjoy the aerobic benefits of swimming.

One good exercise for strengthening the chest or pectoral muscles is the press-up (or push-up). Do three sets of five press-ups or less to start with, and increase the number of repetitions as your strength increases.

Next lie on your back with your knees bent slightly and your feet placed, if necessary, under something to keep them down. Put your hands behind your head and do some sit-ups. This exercise works the upper abdominal muscles and so helps trim your stomach and waistline. However, sit-ups are tough to do so start with two sets of five repetitions. As time goes by gradually increase the number of both. To work the side upper abdominal muscles, alternately touch one elbow to the opposite knee as you sit up.

In between sets of sit-ups you can further work your chest muscles by lying back on the floor, putting your arms straight out from your sides, then raising them to bring them parallel to each other above you. Repeat this ten times. Hold a book in each hand to give yourself some more weight to lift if you wish. You can also raise your arms forwards from beside your head. These exercises also work the shoulder muscles.

Because Cancer is the only zodiac sign ruled by the Moon, you can extend these exercises by adding those given for the other two signs of the Water triplicity, namely Scorpio (see Tuesday) and Pisces (see Thursday).

TUESDAY: This is the day of Mars, which rules both Aries and Scorpio, so on Tuesdays you should concentrate on exercising your face and head, and your genitals. As these exercises are necessarily limited, you can also take a brisk walk or do some other aerobic activity if you wish.

First give your scalp a massage, then exercise the muscles of your face by alternately contracting and relaxing them, starting with your forehead and working down to the chin. Next massage the edge of your jaw in a circular motion with your fingers, starting beneath the ears and working downwards until you reach a point below your eyes. Then work back to the ears. Do this three more times. The massage stimulates the flow of the sex hormone testosterone and thereby improves your sex drive. Now give your hair a shampoo and a nettle scalp rub (see page 51), followed by a facial cleansing and a recommended face pack (see page 52).

The best exercise for the sexual organs, namely sexual intercourse, requires a partner and should be done at least once today, if not more often. Love making is not usually regarded as an exercise, but in fact it is and a good one too, working as it does the heart and lungs and several muscle groups, while at the same time relieving tensions and providing emotional and sexual satisfaction. Those who are single should masturbate; it is no longer regarded as a mortal sin or the destroyer of moral fibre as it once was. Nor does it cause hairs to grow on the palms of the hands.

WEDNESDAY: Wednesday is ruled by Mercury, as are the zodiac signs Gemini and Virgo. Gemini governs the chest and lungs, and the hands, arms and shoulders. Virgo rules the abdomen, which includes the muscles of the lower abdomen.

These are the body areas that you must work on today. Both signs also have rulership over the nervous system.

Because Mercury governs locomotion, today is an excellent day to go for a brisk walk (or a jog), in order to exercise your heart and lungs. Deep breathing in the fresh air will also benefit you. If circumstances prevent you from going outside, try indoor running on the spot or, better still, skipping.

Arm strength can be built up by doing more sets of press-ups; these will also work your shoulder and chest muscles. Do some lateral arm raises to increase your shoulder strength. Begin by standing up straight with your feet together and your arms by your sides. Now raise your arms outwards sideways until they are level with your shoulders. Breathe in as you do this. Count to five, then lower them, breathing out at the same time. Repeat this ten times. Next raise your arms forwards, breathing in again, and hold them while you count to five, then breathe out. You can increase the workload by holding a book (or dumbell) in each hand.

Press-ups are effective in strengthening the triceps, or the upper and outer arm muscles, which straighten the arms. The biceps can be worked by standing up straight holding a fairly heavy book or dumbell in each hand, then bending your arms to bring them up to your shoulders, breathing in as you do so then out as you straighten your arms. Repeat five or six times to complete a set. Do three sets altogether. Far more strenuous biceps exercise is provided by taking hold of the outside top of a door frame (or an overhead beam) and pulling yourself up to touch your chin to its undersurface, although such chin-ups are not recommended unless you are already strong and fit.

Next, improve your hand strength by squeezing a tennis ball. Change hands after squeezing the ball five times with one hand. Aim to work up to three sets with each hand.

The Virgo-ruled lower abdominal muscles are ideally exercised by lying on your back with your legs out straight, putting your hands behind your head, and then raising your legs to an upright position, breathing in as you do so. Lower your legs and breathe out. Repeat five more times, then take a break and do two more sets. Increase the repetitions as your tummy muscles strengthen. Longer-legged men will find the exercise much easier to do by reaching back to take hold of the under-surface of something heavy like a chest of drawers. This stops their upper body from lifting as they try to raise their legs.

THURSDAY: The ruler of Thursday, and of Sagittarius and Pisces, is Jupiter. Today you must therefore concentrate on exercising your hips, thighs and feet.

Because Sagittarius belongs, like the Sun, to the Fire tri-plicity, Thursday is another day on which you can to do some aerobic exercise, so do try to take a brisk 20 minute walk. Apart from its beneficial effect on the lungs and the heart, walking exercises the shoulders, the hips, the legs and the feet, the last three being areas that you need to work on today. If you prefer you can go cycling or jogging; cycling is particu-larly good exercise for the hips and thighs.

When you return from your walk, or before you go cycling or jogging, work on your hips and thighs by doing two or three sets of knee raises. Stand up straight with your feet together, raise one knee to hip height, lower it, then raise the other. Repeat the sequence for another nine times. Do more sets if you can.

Next stand with your legs about 12 inches apart and your hands on your hips. Now lower your body by bending at the knees until your thighs are parallel with the floor, keeping your head up. Then straighten up again. Repeat these squats six times to complete a set. Do one or two more sets if you can. As time goes by increase the number of sets and repeti-tions.

Next, stand side-on to a wall, balance yourself against it with your hand and lift the outside leg sideways, until it is parallel with the floor. Then let it fall and repeat another five times. Now change over and exercise the other hip joint and thigh in the same way. Do two more sets with each leg. These leg raises can also be done by lying on your side on the floor.

Now lie face down on your bed with your feet and lower legs projecting over its edge. From the straight position, bend your legs upright from the knees ten times to complete one set. Try to do two more sets. This exercise works the rear thigh muscles; the effort required can be increased by trying to bend your legs against your partner's gentle, but firm, resisting pull.

Spend as much time as you can today walking about the house with bare or stockinged feet, thereby giving your toes the opportunity to spread and separate. Ask your partner to give you a foot massage, and attend to any corns or callouses. Trim away hard skin, and soften and protect your feet with a good skin cream. Make sure that you cut your toe-nails, if necessary, straight across to prevent them growing inwards. Always visit your chiropodist or pedicurist on a Thursday whenever possible.

FRIDAY: This is the day of Venus, which also rules Taurus and Libra. Taurus governs, for our purposes, the neck, and Libra the lower back and the buttocks. These are the areas of your body on which you will work today.

First, stand up straight and give your neck muscles a general warm-up by rolling your head. This is done by slowly letting your head loll forward, then turn it to look at one side, keep rotating it to look up at the ceiling, continue the movement to look at the other side of you, then bring your head back to its first downward-looking position. Repeat two or three times, then reverse the direction of movement. Continue the exercise for about five minutes.

Next lie across your bed on your stomach with your head sticking out over one side of it. Now drop your head, then raise it up to stare ahead. Repeat this five times, then relax before doing another two sets. This exercise strengthens the muscles at the back of the neck. You can then work those at the front of your neck by turning over on your back, letting your head fall back so you look at the wall, and then raise it until your chin touches your chest. Do three sets of five repetitions to start with.

The lower back and buttock muscles can be exercised by first standing up straight with your feet apart and your hands behind your head. Now lower your body forwards until it is parallel with the ground, keeping your head up to look straight ahead as you do this. Then slowly raise yourself to the upright position. Repeat five more times. Do more sets as your back strength increases. The buttock muscles can also usefully be exercised by standing up straight and tightening them. Keep the muscles contracted for a slow count of five. Then relax for a couple of seconds and repeat. Do this fifteen times.

Now work your lower back muscles at the side by putting your hands on your hips and leaning over sideways, first one side then the other. Repeat five more times to complete a set. Relax for a few moments before doing two more sets. This exercise will help to trim your waist.

The following back and buttock exercise is more strenuous than the first and must be done with care. Lie on your stomach on the floor and put your hands behind your head. Now try to lift both your stomach and your legs as far as you can from the ground, so that you form a sort of arch between your upper chest and your feet. Hold the raised position for two or three seconds, then relax. Repeat five more times. Do more sets as your strength increases.

SATURDAY: Saturday is ruled by Saturn, as are the zodiac signs Capricorn and Aquarius, which means that the body parts to be exercised today are the knees and the lower legs. These are best worked by walking, especially up hills or stairs, which also has the effect of increasing the blood supply to the legs. Cycling or jogging may be done if preferred.

You can further strengthen the calves by standing with your legs together, then raising yourself up on tiptoe. Then drop your heels to the floor and repeat. Continue until your calf muscles are fatigued. In a similar way, you can exercise the muscles at the front of your legs by raising your toes from the ground at the ankle then lowering them. You may need to hold on to something to keep your balance. Again, carry on for as long as you can.

If you wish you can do the squat exercise described for Thursday, as this also works the knees.

Lastly, as Capricorn is the ruler of the skin, cleanse your skin and relax by taking a long hot bath. Afterwards apply a skin lotion to soften your skin. Then go out and enjoy yourself. Any physical exercise like dancing will be good for you, although do try not to drink and smoke too much, if at all. Remember that tomorrow brings the start of another Zodiac Work-out Schedule, continuing the dawn of a new you.

Combating Stress

The biggest enemy of your looks and your sense of well-being in the modern world is stress. Stress is caused by those happenings around you that make you tense, frustrated, angry or unhappy, which in other words shock the system, although even happy events like a marriage, a birth, or a holiday, can be stressful and thus physically and psychologically damaging to you.

The greatest stress is caused by major negative life upheavals such as divorce, a death in the family, the loss of one's job, or a serious accident, which may take you weeks, months or even years to recover from completely. Yet the ordinary day-to-day stress caused by noise, long journeys to work, crowds and traffic, pressure to meet deadlines, family problems, and insufficient money for your needs, can not only raise your blood pressure and pulse rate, but lead to your suffering from irritability, insomnia, loss of appetite and weight, and depression. And these bodily disturbances may be the precursors to far more serious health breakdowns in the form of diabetes, heart attacks, and cancer.

However, the twelve zodiac types do react somewhat differently to stress. It is, in a general sense, less harmful to those born under Aries, Leo and Sagittarius, the signs of the Fire triplicity, or that have one of these signs rising. These people are the most active, ambitious and worldly of the twelve zodiac types and may, at least in the short term, actually thrive on stress. This is particularly true for the cardinal Ariens and the mutable Sagittarians, but less so for the fixed Leos, who not only have problems coping with uncertainty but are particularly prone to heart attacks. Leos can and do enjoy fighting their way to the top but once they are there they need to feel completely secure. Redundancy or dislodgement by a rival can shatter them, and that, to a Leo, may prove fatal.

Stress is perhaps most harmful to those born under Gemini, Libra and Aquarius, which together make up the Air triplicity, or those who have these signs rising. They are the thinkers of the zodiac, preferring as they do to live by their wits and their mental talents, which make them vulnerable to anything that disturbs their mental composure. The Air signs typically worry unnecessarily, which in itself is stressful, particularly as they often magnify the difficulties they are facing. Mutable Geminis are most at risk from stress, for they have a somewhat fragile nervous system and delicate lungs. High stress levels may encourage them to smoke too much and to eat improperly, which can result in lung diseases or in eating disorders like bulimia, or even cause them to have a mental breakdown. Libras deal with stress, where possible, by avoiding it, but if this cannot be done they are vulnerable, like Geminis, to mental breakdown. The fixed Aquarians are better grounded psychologically than either Geminis or Libras, which gives them a slight advantage in dealing with stress, yet they cannot cope with anything that affects them emotionally. In fact emotional stress is far more dangerous to their health than any mental concern. Indeed, Aquarians, like Leos, are prone to strokes and heart attacks.

The Earth sign triplicity of Taurus, Virgo and Capricorn also have special problems with stress, for those born under these signs, or who have them rising, both love and need stability in their lives, hence stress, which undermines certainty, can be very damaging to them. Indeed, the Earth signs, like Libras, deal with stress where possible by avoiding it, preferring as they do the quiet life, making their advances slowly and steadily. Yet of the three, Virgos are most at risk from stress, for they have the weakest and most sensitive nervous system. In this respect, as in the fact they are born worriers, they resemble Geminis. Taureans will silently suffer stress if they cannot avoid it, while hoping that it will go away, yet if it persists they will be driven to extremes of anger and frustration, which may result in violence being offered to those responsible for it. The Capricorn-born avoid stress by working behind the scenes, striving, like Scorpios, for long-term goals rather than short-term victories. But if they are robbed of their final triumph they will then completely go to pieces, losing both self-respect and self-confidence, which may result in them destroying themselves with drink or drugs, or even by committing suicide.

Those born under the Water signs of Cancer, Scorpio and Pisces, or who have one of these signs rising, while being emotionally sensitive, have a surprisingly high tolerance to stress, due largely to the fact that they can more easily express their hurt and disquiet than the other sign types. Both sexes are able to cry quite easily (which acts as a safety valve), and have little difficulty in talking about their problems. And being naturally sympathetic and caring people themselves, they are aided by the wide circle of friends and confidants they often have, who will listen to them when they need it. Like the elements for which they are named, Water people are able to go with the flow, and to either absorb or work their way around that which is stressful to others. The more intense and secretive Scorpios are perhaps most at risk, for while they can appear to be unaffected by stress for a long time, when they reach breaking point they suddenly crumble and collapse, revealed as they then are to have feet of clay.

Stress is best dealt with by avoiding it where possible. But because considerable stress is caused by not only sad but happy events, such as marriage, giving birth, and starting a new job, which few would wish to miss out on, it is important to stagger these happenings as far as possible, in order to reduce the total amount of stress you experience at any one time. And when something unfortunate does happen, like a death in the family, try not to compound its harmful effects by moving house or by changing your job soon afterwards.

However, you can certainly reduce the average, day-to-day stress in your life by working shorter hours, by not taking on more than you can reasonably handle, by sharing your responsibilities, and by talking over your difficulties with your colleagues and friends. You can also reduce stress by eating proper meals at a regular time, and by sitting down to eat them; by not talking shop when you do so; by leaving home for work, or your office for appointments, in good time, so that you are less bothered by the inevitable traffic hold-ups and are not tempted to drive too fast or too recklessly; by avoiding frequent travel by plane; by getting to bed early; by having some hobbies or interests unrelated to your work; by taking a walk in the evenings with your partner; by stopping smoking and by reducing the amount of alcohol you drink; by dieting if you are over-weight; and by having reasonable expectations for yourself and your family. Where the last is concerned, remember that it is very stressful to be always reaching for the stars!

5

Career Choices

A tradesman who would succeed in his way must begin by
establishing a character of integrity and good manners; without the former, nobody will go to the shop at all; without the
latter, nobody will go there twice . . . It is the same in higher
life, and in the great business of the world. A man who does
not solidly establish and really deserve a character of truth,
probity, good manners, and good morals, at his first setting out
in the world, may impose and shine like a meteor for a very
short time, but will very soon vanish, and be extinguished
with contempt.

From *Lord Chesterfield's Letters to his Son*

To THOSE who have to work, which includes most of us,
choosing the right job or career is very important, for we
not only make our livelihood from our work but also derive
much of our sense of self and our happiness from it. Our work,
in other words, helps to define us as individuals, which is why
those without jobs often feel alienated from society and why
being employed is prized, not simply for the wages it provides,
but for its psychological benefits.

And because the job or career that we select, if we are fortunate enough to have a choice, ideally suits our personality, it
is hardly surprising that those born under the same zodiac sign
are attracted to certain types of job, which are often quite different from those preferred by people born under another sign.
This is why I shall describe in this chapter the character of
persons born under each sign and give a representative selection of the sorts of job most suited to them. I hope this will
help you to pick the right occupation for yourself, if you are

either not yet employed or feel dissatisfied with the work you are doing.

However, do remember that as everyone's character is symbolised (or created) by both the Sun sign and the rising sign, you must read what is said about both signs, if they are different, to obtain a better insight into your own personality and to know what jobs are best for you. You should also, if you are a cuspal type, read the characteristics of the adjacent sign as some of them will likewise apply to you. You will, in either case, be something of a mixture where your character traits and job preferences are concerned. But if your Sun sign and rising sign are the same, which makes you a double Aries, a double Libra or whatever, and if you were not born on the cusp, then you should find that the description offered for that sign is exact.

Aries, The Ram

Aries people, being the most independent zodiac type, are natural leaders and path-finders. They hate taking orders, but relish giving them, and can only be happy in a supervisory capacity, or, better still, running the entire show. Yet they are both doers and thinkers, who can unite their energy and intellect to achieve their goals. While they are better at the short burst then the long haul, their interest and drive can be kept alive by recognition and applause. For Arians love the spotlight. Success and accomplishment are their ultimate thrill, which is why they can never be happy in jobs that offer no challenge or reward. They are not, as it were, hewers of wood or drawers of water, but what they do must be on their own terms for they cannot stand to be driven, and will often leave an otherwise good job if put under pressure. Arians usually have plenty of ideas (which may or may not be their own), a lot to say and advice to give, and plenty of enthusiasm when their interest is fired. Yet they are often overly touchy, aggressive, impulsive and jealous, which makes them difficult to get along with. They are also prone to exaggeration, and in order not to be outdone or outshone will claim the honours when they are not rightfully theirs. Nobody puts self-interest first more than Arians. They are people driven by ego.

Suitable Aries careers: actor, agent (literary and otherwise), advertising executive, animal trainer, anthropologist, architect, barber, butcher, carpenter, chemist, designer, doctor, explorer, firefighter, football player, forester, gunsmith, journalist, lifeguard, neurologist, novelist, public relations consultant, salesperson, scientist, slaughterer, soldier, stockbroker, surgeon, surveyor, travel guide, zoo keeper, zoologist.

Taurus, The Bull

Taurus people are essentially cautious types who like to know where they are going and who do not relish changes or new ideas. They are traditionalists, needing to keep one foot in the past while reluctantly pushing the other into the future. They are good with their hands, patient, and determined, which are traits that incline them to practical occupations, especially those that are carried on out of doors. Yet they also often have both a love of, and a talent for, art and music, most notably for the plastic arts and for musical performance. They can be very stubborn, they like their own way, and they are resistant to anything novel or innovative. Thus once they have made up their minds they are reluctant to change their opinion or course. Yet they are sociable, warm, and generally easy-going, which makes them good team members, if not team leaders, as they are never entirely happy when required to make decisions. The Taurus-born are, however, adverse to being bossed or ordered about, so those in command can only get the best out of them by persuasion, never by coercion. But they do need supervision, as they are naturally slothful and indolent. As they are neither intellectually quick nor particularly adaptable, Taurus people function best in those jobs that require a formal training or an apprenticeship and which call upon them to do more or less the same thing, day in day out.

Suitable Taurus careers: accountant, actor, architect, banker, beautician, bodyguard, bookmaker, botanist, builder, cashier, chef, chemist, choreographer, church minister, engineer, engraver, estate agent, factory worker, farmer/farm labourer, florist, gardener, groundsman, hairdresser, historian, masseur/masseuse, metallurgist, musician, nurse, pawnbroker, paediatrician, political scientist, publican, recording engineer, shop assistant, singer, stone mason.

Gemini, The Twins

Gemini people are distinguished by their quick wits and ready tongues, which make them excellent communicators or persuaders. They are particularly suited for any job which requires these talents, especially if it calls upon them to use their charm and bright humour. Geminians are also opinionated, yet seldom have much depth to their knowledge, being very much surface people, and thus tend to fare best in those careers which call for native cunning and mental gymnastics rather than profound thought. They are quickly bored by routine, find it difficult to master details, and although good at coming up with ideas have less success with putting them into practice. Basically outgoing, lively and interesting, particularly with those who make no demands upon their emotions, they are adaptable and resourceful, enjoy changes and challenges, yet are prone to anxiety and self-doubt when the going gets tough. Geminians are most vulnerable when anything involving both mind and emotions comes under attack, such as the running of a business, when they are susceptible to ulcers and mental breakdown. They are good with words and figures, at arranging displays and shows, at understanding technology, and at keeping others interested and amused. But they are fickle and flighty, seldom staying long in any one job, particularly as they are easily flattered and tempted by rivals. They can have sharp tongues, and when upset can be unkind, scornful and unmerciful.

Suitable Gemini careers: actor, advertising executive, architect, auctioneer, barrister, bookseller, business executive, church minister, computer operator, copy writer, courier, demonstrator, diplomat, disc jockey, editor, engineer, electrician, fashion designer, illustrator, inventor, government official, journalist, lecturer, lyricist, political economist, public relations executive, salesperson, secretary, solicitor, teacher, travel agent, writer.

Cancer, The Crab

Cancer people, while emotionally sensitive and easily hurt, are physically tough and make reliable, hard working and loyal employees. They enjoy working both with and for others, and are often attracted to the caring professions. Indeed, their natural warmth, understanding and compassion make them ideally suited to such work. They dislike any job, however, that is strictly routine or that requires them to operate machinery. They possess a rich imagination and are often creative, attributes that can be put to good use in fields like advertising and design, especially when the products or results are aimed at the home. In business and commerce they function best by feeling their way, rather than by thinking things through logically. Yet the Cancer-born are seldom ambitious for money or fame, preferring instead a more feet-on-the-ground, mundane existence, although they are usually very good at organising and enthusing others. However, once they have decided upon a course of action they are very tenacious and determined, which traits of course can bring them success. They have a very good sense of value and worth, which along with their keen eye for colour and form, make them excellent buyers, home decorators, and display artists. While they often know what to buy, they are reluctant to spend large sums of money, being naturally careful with it. A love of the sea inclines Cancer-people towards a career in the Royal or merchant navy, or to employment on the beach or shore.

Suitable Cancer careers: antiquarian, architect, archaeologist, artist, bartender, barrister, brewer, buyer, chef, cleaner, church minister, designer, doctor, ethnologist, ferry-operator, fisherman, harbour master, home help, historian, hotel keeper, journalist, child carer, obstetrician, political scientist, politician, probation officer, publican, librarian, life-guard, midwife, nurse, physiotherapist, sailor, secretary, shop assistant, social worker, steward, tailor, waiter, writer.

Leo, The Lion

Leo people have many qualities that make them ideal employees, such as reliability, loyalty, industry, and honesty, yet these are only fully displayed, and Leos at their happiest, when they cease to be humble workers, and becomes the boss. For Leos love to be in command. They feel that it is their birthright to be giving out orders and to be at the hub or centre of things. They can seldom be fulfilled by lowly employment, but ever aspire to make something of themselves and to shine, because it is only when heads turn in their direction that they feel worthwhile and secure. But while hard working, Leos shy away from physical labour, preferring instead to put in long hours in white-collar jobs, with their hands on the helm. Yet although it is power, and not wealth, that forms the basis of their ambition, they always expect their salaries to be commensurate with their position. They are excellent organisers and usually enjoy good relations with their colleagues and subordinates.

Leos can bear disappointment with fortitude, and be stimulated to try harder. Indeed, they seldom give up once their energies have been focussed, and will remain loyal to a particular company or organisation unless lured away by an offer of more power or status. They may have somewhat fixed views, however, as the opinions and ideas of their youth tend to remain unchanged as they age. At their best Leos are just and fair, and are quite prepared to fight for the rights of others; while at their worst they are pompous and overbearing, and forever telling others what to do.

Suitable Leo careers: academic, actor, army officer, artist, barrister, banker, business executive, cardiologist, civil servant, consultant, doctor, editor, entertainer, factory foreman or forewoman, fashion model, film/theatre director, goldsmith, impresario, lecturer, palace official, police officer, political scientist, politician, public relations consultant, manager, teacher, social worker, solicitor, union official.

Virgo, The Virgin

Virgo people enjoy any work that permits them to use their brains, for they are like the typical Gemini, mental rather than physical types. They prefer dealing with the details, especially if they involve mathematics and calculation, rather than the overall plan, and will work conscientiously and hard to get things right. They are excellent analysts and organisers, and are happy to tackle any problem providing they are given sufficient time and encouragement. For Virgoans do not like to be rushed or pressured, and their anxious disposition and lack of self-esteem make them particularly vulnerable, in stressful conditions, to ulcers and nervous breakdowns. Yet given the right circumstances and sufficient support, they can do wonders.

Virgoans are honest and honourable, with a strong sense of duty, although they have little patience with those who are slower than themselves or whose habits are less fastidious than their own. They are rarely late, seldom slack, and would not dream of leaving work early, so when in positions of authority they expect the same commitment and high standards from everybody else, so they can become slave-drivers. They measure themselves by what they know, which is why they constantly try to improve their educational standing by taking courses and night classes. They love words and their meaning, and the power of expression that they give. Hence they are particularly attracted to any work that calls on them to talk and explain, or which requires analysis and investigation skills.

Suitable Virgo careers: accountant, author, banker, book-keeper, chemist, clerk, critic, decorator, detective, designer, film editor, gardener, graphic artist, historian, horologist, librarian, laboratory assistant, linguist, market researcher, mathematician, negotiator, neurologist, ophthalmologist, orthopaedist, presenter, publisher's assistant, researcher, restorer, secretary, speech writer, stockbroker, teacher, veterinarian.

Libra, The Balance

Libra people work best as part of a team rather than alone, for they not only have difficulty in making decisions and in planning ahead, but may too easily be corrupted by power. Their open and friendly manner makes them well suited to working with the public, especially as their innate diplomacy is very useful in helping to calm tempers and deal with complaints. Having an interest in clothes and fashion, they are attracted to jobs like hairdressing and clothes design that involve improving the appearance of others. In fact Librans of both sexes are commonly found behind the counters of beauticians and of health shops. They are also interested in the arts and often have talents in that direction, which may take them on to the stage or into some other branch of entertainment. Typically they have a talent for music. Their strong sense of justice and good negotiating skills make them excellent adjudicators, particularly as they seldom become emotionally involved with either the cause or the disputants, even though they can only guide those concerned to a conclusion, not make it themselves. Few Librans like getting their hands dirty, so any job that calls on them to roll up their sleeves and reach for a shovel is not for them. They dislike arguments and any sort of upset or disharmony, thus they can only be happy when their surroundings are orderly and pleasant and their fellow workers reasonable and uncontentious. They are intelligent and eager to learn, yet often changeable, capricious and sulky, sometimes even depressive.

Suitable Libra careers: actor, ambassador, antique dealer, artist, bartender, barrister, beautician, chemist, church minister, diplomat, engraver, entertainer, fashion designer, hairdresser, jeweller, librarian, manicurist, mediator, milliner, musician, painter, physicist, politician, public relations consultant, publisher, salesperson, scientist, secretary, social worker, sociologist, teacher, toy-maker, trainer, writer.

Scorpio, The Scorpion

Scorpio people have many attributes that make them excellent employees. These include industry, punctuality, honesty, and concern with detail. They are also very determined and resourceful once their interest has been aroused, and their quiet, persistent and often subtle manner helps them overcome opposition and can take them right to the top, especially as they seldom expect instant success but are prepared to work long and hard for it. They are very curious and analytical, and are fascinated by all puzzles and mysteries, which explains why many Scorpios are attracted to, and do well in, the detective branch of the police force, scientific research, and in uncovering the secrets of the earth. Their well-developed intuitive powers likewise enable them to become good psychiatrists. It is rare for Scorpios to be preoccupied with making money, even though they want to be well rewarded for what they do, for they love and need mental stimulation. Their work has to interest them. While they often appear strong and capable, and may, in their relationships with colleagues and inferiors, seem overly direct and harsh, their manner is more of a pose than reality, because inwardly they are very sensitive, being easily hurt, and full of self-doubt. This discrepancy between the inner and the outer person produces the tension and psychological stress felt by many Scorpios, and accounts for their desire for power. Being the boss not only gives Scorpios a sanctum in which to hide, but means that there is no-one looking over their shoulder and criticising them.

Suitable Scorpio careers: accountant, archaeologist, author, biologist, brewer, butcher, chemist, detective, diver, doctor, embalmer, engineer, farmer, firefighter, geologist, hypnotist, inventor, journalist, librarian, mechanic, miner, oil driller, physicist, pilot, police officer, psychiatrist, psychologist, sailor, sanitation engineer, scientist, soldier, stockbroker, systems analyst, undertaker, veterinarian.

Sagittarius, The Centaur

Sagittarius people are outgoing, generally ebullient types who like change and travel, which means that they are rarely happy in a job that offers no variety or challenge and which keeps them stuck in one place. They have a lot of will power, and once they have decided upon their goals will work hard to achieve them. They prefer to work with others rather than alone, but as they dislike being told what to do, they function best as managers or executives, calling the shots and giving the orders while being part of the team. In this capacity they are helped by their excellent organising ability and natural enthusiasm. Indeed, few are better at motivating others than a Sagittarian.

Sagittarians love the outdoors, sport and animals, a combination of interests that sees many of them employed as gamekeepers, riding instructors, horse breeders and, being attracted to gambling, bookmakers. They enjoy teaching and instructing others, for like the other Fire signs they love to be the centre of attention and in charge of the show, although typically they hide their own psychological needs behind a mass of verbiage about the importance of education and the raising of moral standards. While they are generous and giving, their prodigality in this respect is often directed at those who can help them in their career. Thus they are frequently hypocritical and self-seeking, flattering those who can do them good with both words and largesse.

Suitable Sagittarius careers: advertising executive, bookmaker, builder, civil engineer, civil servant, church minister, counsellor, courier, editor, entertainer, farmer, fund raiser, gamekeeper, grocer, groom, horse breeder, insurance agent, journalist, lawyer, magistrate, manager, musician, politician, representative, salesperson, school principal, singer, sports instructor, teacher, theatre manager, travel agent, translator, union official, university professor.

Capricorn, The Goat

Capricorn people are stable, reliable, hard working and dependable types, who want to do well in their job but are happier making slow and steady progress towards their goals, rather than scrabbling for early success. In fact Capricorns are often unnerved if they achieve their ambitions too soon as their life is thereby robbed of direction and purpose. They are conservative and dignified and like to know where they are going, what the rules of the game are, and what can be reasonably expected from the enterprise. They are careful to play by the rules, realising as they do that their sheer plodding determination is very hard to beat. Capricorns are careful with money, preferring to save it or invest it rather than spend it, but all too often, however, their prudence is seen as meanness. They are particularly keen on buying land and property, as they like their wealth to have substance that the neighbours can see. Their thrift applies to all things, and they would far rather re-use something than throw it away. But although overly cautious, they are honest and trustworthy, and have a strong sense of duty. Yet Capricornians are not particularly social or self-confident, preferring either a solo career or one where associates are kept at a safe distance. This is perhaps why many Capricorns become professional entertainers or sportsmen, being in the public eye but ever separated from the admiring crowd.

Suitable Capricorn careers: architect, artist, banker, book-keeper, boxer, broker, builder, civil servant, contractor, dentist, dermatologist, editor, electrician, engineer, entertainer (especially singer), estate agent, farmer, funeral director, gravedigger, judge, labourer, lawyer, manager, mathematician, miner, osteopath, plumber, politician, promoter, researcher, school principal, scientist, systems analyst, teacher, technician.

Aquarius, The Water Pourer

Aquarian people are the most independent and unusual of the zodiac types. They have much in common with Capricorns, being basically serious-minded, hard-working, and practical, yet different in that they love the unexpected and the odd, are always ready to drop everything and go off to chase a new dream, and cannot stand any form of restriction. Hence Aquarians are most suited to free-lance occupations or to those that give them much freedom of movement. They enjoy travel and learning about other cultures, and they have an interest in anything strange or occult. Aquarians love to challenge the system, and for this reason can often blow a fresh blast of air through old and outdated ways of procedure. Yet at worst they may become violent revolutionaries, because although they are interested in improving the lot of humanity they often make the mistake of believing that the end justifies the means. They are particularly unusual in that while they habitually love everything new, they also have a real feeing for the past, which is why many Aquarians become historians and archaeologists. In their daily contact with others Aquarians are polite, kind and thoughtful, and always willing to try to see other people's points of view, that is, before incisively rubbishing their arguments. They prefer their own company and so rarely join club or societies for social reasons, especially as small-talk bores them. Typically, they have many acquaintances but few real friends.

Suitable Aquarian careers: actor, antiquarian, archaeologist, astronomer, astrologer, broadcaster, computer programmer, dancer, electrician, electronics engineer, film maker, geologist, graphic artist, historian, journalist, librarian, literary assistant, musician, pilot, photographer, postal worker, producer, psychic researcher, psychologist, publisher, radiographer, railway employee, scientist, singer, surveyor, teacher, technician, television camera-operator, welfare officer, writer.

Pisces, The Fish

Pisces people are pleasant, sympathetic and generally inoffensive types, who both understand and get on well with other people. They are good listeners, which makes them well suited for any type of counselling work, although they are less able to take care of their own lives. Many Pisceans enter the medical profession, as they love to serve and succour others. Their natural friendliness, good humour and desire to create a favourable impression, help make them successful in working with the public, most notably in hotels and restaurants and in the tourist industry. They are often good cooks and knowledgeable about food; they certainly enjoy eating it. Pisces people have a well-developed intuition, which enables them to divine the character and motives of others, and their psychic gifts may be sufficiently outstanding to allow them to become mediums or clairvoyants. It is unusual for them to be particularly ambitious, although they are prone to fantasizing about their potential. They tend to lack motivation and resourcefulness, and usually require the assistance of someone with a stronger and more forceful personality in order to become materially successful. They make eager students and researchers, valuing knowledge and learning as they do. They work methodically and in an orderly way. An interest in the arts, coupled with artistic talents and a good imagination, often naturally directs the Pisces-born into this field, either as performers or creators.

Suitable Pisces careers: accountant, antiquarian, archaeologist, astrologer, bartender, biologist, bookkeeper, caterer, chemist, chiropodist, chiropractor, church minister, doctor, geologist, hair stylist, herbalist, hospital worker, hotelier, hydrologist, librarian, literary assistant, oceanographer, medium, musician, nurse, politician, researcher, sailor, secretary, social worker, teacher, waiter, writer, veterinarian.

Most astrologers would say that if you were born under one of the Fire signs (Aries, Leo and Sagittarius) or under one of the Air signs (Gemini, Libra and Aquarius), you are more likely to make progress in the world, perhaps to the extent of becoming rich and famous, than if you were born under one of the Earth signs (Taurus, Virgo and Capricorn) or under one of the Water signs (Cancer, Scorpio and Pisces), due to the fact you have more energy and ambition.

But any reader of Aesop's fable about the tortoise and the hare will know that the race is not always won by the swift, nor, for that matter, the battle by the strong. Patience and good old-fashioned determination can often triumph over the fast and the furious, for those who dazzle with their brilliance may just as quickly fizzle out.

This is certainly borne out by one group of men who reached the highest position possible in their society, namely American presidents. An analysis of their birth dates reveals that the largest number of them were born under Water signs, with those born under Earth signs following along not too far behind:

President	Date of birth	Sun sign
1) George Washington	22-02-1732	Pisces*
2) John Adams	30-10-1735	Scorpio
3) Thomas Jefferson	13-04-1743	Aries
4) James Madison	16-03-1751	Pisces
5) James Monroe	28-04-1758	Taurus
6) John Quincy Adams	11-07-1767	Cancer
7) Andrew Jackson	15-03-1767	Pisces
8) Martin Van Buren	05-12-1782	Sagittarius

(* = Cuspal type)

President	Date of birth	Sun sign
9) William H. Harrison	09-02-1773	Aquarius
10) John Tyler	29-03-1790	Aries
11) James K. Polk	02-11-1795	Scorpio
12) Zachary Taylor	24-11-1784	Sagittarius
13) Milliard Fillmore	07-01-1800	Capricorn
14) Franklin Pierce	23-11-1804	Sagittarius*
15) James Buchanan	23-04-1791	Taurus*
16) Abraham Lincoln	12-02-1809	Aquarius
17) Andrew Johnson	29-12-1808	Capricorn
18) Ulysses S. Grant	27-04-1822	Taurus
19) Rutherford B. Hayes	04-10-1822	Libra
20) James A. Garfield	19-11-1831	Scorpio
21) Chester A. Arthur	05-10-1830	Libra
22) Grover Cleveland	18-03-1837	Pisces*
23) Benjamin Harrison	20-04-1833	Aries*
24) Grover Cleveland	as above	
25) William McKinley	29-01-1843	Aquarius
26) Theodore Roosevelt	27-10-1858	Scorpio
27) William Howard Taft	15-09-1857	Virgo
28) Woodrow Wilson	29-12-1856	Capricorn
29) Warren G. Harding	02-11-1865	Scorpio
30) Calvin Coolidge	04-07-1872	Cancer
31) Herbert C. Hoover	10-08-1874	Leo
32) Franklin D. Roosevelt	30-01-1882	Aquarius
33) Harry S. Truman	08-05-1884	Taurus
34) Dwight D. Eisenhower	14-10-1890	Libra
35) John F. Kennedy	29-05-1917	Gemini
36) Lyndon B. Johnson	27-08-1908	Virgo
37) Richard M. Nixon	09-01-1913	Capricorn
38) Gerald Ford	14-07-1913	Cancer
39) Jimmy Carter	01-10-1924	Libra
40) Ronald Reagan	06-02-1911	Aquarius
41) George Bush	12-06-1924	Gemini
42) William Clinton	19-08-1946	Leo

(* = Cuspal type)

This list of 41 individuals who have become president of the United States (Grover Cleveland was both the 22nd and the 24th president), shows that while the largest number born under any one zodiac sign is five, this was achieved by two sign types, Aquarius (an Air sign) and Scorpio (a Water sign), who together make up one-quarter of the total. They are closely followed by two Earth sign types, Taurus and Capricorn, one Air sign, Libra, and another Water sign, Pisces, who have each produced four presidents. Coincidentally, the first American president, George Washington, was born under the Water sign Pisces, just as the first Roman emperor, Julius Caesar, was born under another, namely Cancer. Indeed, it is curious to note that when the Roman empire fell to the Goths in AD 423, it was led by Honorius, the 42nd emperor, and that the United States, the latest superpower, which has taken over much that is Roman in its system of government (e.g. the Capitol, the Senate) and symbols of office (such as the eagle), is now led by its 42nd president, Bill Clinton. Could this be an ominous omen for both him and the United States? Or will that country's the possible downfall or collapse take place instead under whoever succeeds him, who will be the 42nd person to actually reach this august office? Only time will tell if the numerical association is merely coincidental or forebodingly meaningful.

The table below shows how all the signs fared:

Zodiac sign	Number becoming president
Scorpio	5
Aquarius	5
Taurus	4
Libra	4
Capricorn	4
Pisces	4
Aries	3
Cancer	3
Sagittarius	3

Gemini	2
Leo	2
Virgo	2

If we compare the signs by their triplicity, it is clear that those born under the Water signs are the most successful at becoming president, while the Fire signs are the least successful, as the following table reveals:

Triplicity	Number becoming president
Water signs	12
Air signs	11
Earth signs	10
Fire signs	8

This means that you need have nothing to worry about if you were born under one of the supposedly disadvantaged Water or Earth signs. You *can* get right to the top. Surprisingly, it is the aggressive and ambitious Fire signs that appear to be the most handicapped, perhaps because while they want to succeed and become the boss, they are hindered from doing so by their lack of patience and perseverance.

So go for it!

6

Your Future Spouse

A man of taste and delicacy marries a woman because he loves
her more than any other. A woman of equal taste and delicacy
marries him because she esteems him, and because he gives
her that preference.

From A *Father's Legacy To His Daughters* by Dr Gregory

PERHAPS THE two most frequently asked questions of astrologers are: 'When shall I marry?' and 'What will my husband (or wife) be like?' For even in these grey days of one-
parent families and increasing marital breakdown, the yearn-
ing for a stable, happy marriage remains strong.

Your birth chart or horoscope can of course give you the
answers to these two questions, and it can also tell you if your
union is likely to be happy. But the astrologer of today must
always take into account the changes in society's attitudes to
marriage. Until about 1965 virtually every couple who wanted
to set up home together, married, whereas nowadays many
couples live together, often happily and successfully, without
doing so. This is why such common-law unions must be brack-
eted with the legally married, although certain astrological
types, especially those born with the Sun in Aquarius or
Gemini, or with these signs rising, are more likely to prefer a
freer relationship than others.

When a birth chart is constructed, the astrologer not only
marks on it the placement of the planets within the zodiac at
the moment of the client's birth, but shows how these relate
to the 'houses'. The houses are twelve imaginary sectors,
which together symbolise all human life, with each house
representing certain aspects of it. For example, the first house

of your chart reveals your physical characteristics and your constitution, your way of behaving, and your likes, dislikes and peculiarities. The cusp or first border of this house is formed by the ascendant and the remaining houses circle around from it in an anti-clockwise order, rather like the spaces between the spokes of a wheel. This is why your rising sign gives such an important insight into your appearance and personality, one normally as great, if not greater, than that provided by your Sun sign.

Directly opposite to the first house is the seventh house, which is the house of marriage, although it also symbolises your sexual desires, and, according to some astrologers, your diplomatic skills, as well as the strangers and any opponents that will come into your life. Where marriage is concerned, the seventh house describes the appearance and character of your spouse, the happiness and general quality of your marriage, and whether or not it is likely to last.

The sign that lies on the cusp of your seventh house indicates the nature of the person that you will either marry or live with. For example, if you were born with Taurus rising the sign of the cusp of your seventh house is Scorpio. Hence your husband (or wife) will have the appearance and character of a Scorpio, which means he will probably have a Scorpio ascendant, or perhaps even his Sun in Scorpio.

The table below shows which zodiac signs are seventh from each other, those on the left being seventh from those opposite them, and vice versa. If you know your time of birth and have found out your rising sign, this will enable you to discover, from the descriptions which follow the table, the appearance and character traits of the person to whom you will commit yourself. The descriptions will also help you to understand your spouse better if you are already married.

Zodiac signs seventh from each other

Aries: Libra
Taurus: Scorpio
Gemini: Sagittarius
Cancer: Capricorn

Leo: Aquarius
Virgo: Pisces

1) If you are a woman with an ascendant in **Aries**, the man you marry will be tall with a strong, well formed body, a broad, roundish face with handsome and regular features (although his nose may be rather large), and blue or light-coloured eyes. His expression will be pleasant and his manner cheerful. His hair will be healthy and shining, worn rather longer than average, and light brown, auburn or possibly black in colour. His complexion, when young, will be smooth and quite soft, with a reddish hue to it, although he is likely to develop certain skin defects and more colour as he ages. He will have little body hair. He will be very particular, possibly even fussy, about his appearance, bathing himself and changing his clothes regularly, and wanting to keep up-to-date with fashion. He will keep his nails clean and his hair combed. He will probably be quite intelligent, and he will be interested in art and music. Indeed, he may have artistic talents of his own. His voice will be pleasant and soothing, and he will generally be kind, considerate and polite. He will have a large circle of friends and he will enjoy social activities. He may even be quite religious. He will treat you with respect and affection, and will be sensitive to your needs. He will have trouble, however, in making decisions and will sometimes try to be all things to all people. Don't expect him to be forceful or masterful, for these traits are not part of his personality. He may be quite idealistic, yet he will also be impractical. Because he will be moved by the plight of others, he may become involved with groups or activities aimed at improving their lot.

If you are male, your wife will probably be blessed with an attractive face and figure, and she will certainly make the best of herself by dressing well and by paying attention to her hair and make-up. However, she may be self-conscious about her thick ankles, which are likely to be her worst feature. She will be a keen if somewhat fastidious housewife, hating mess, untidiness and visible dust. In fact your sloppiness in this regard will be one of the main areas of contention in your relationship. She will love colour and liveliness, which will be a mark of the clothes and furniture she buys, and which she will impart, by her outgoing and bright personality, to all of the many social functions that she will love attending. Be aware that her attractiveness to the opposite sex could make you jealous, especially as she will rather enjoy other men's attention. Yet unfaithfulness will be abhorrent to her, so don't worry unnecessarily. Just remember, however, that she might be driven to cheat if you try to curtail her freedom, which she will hold very dear, to mix and mingle with whomsoever she pleases. She will be interested in the arts, particularly those which combine music and movement, like ballet. In fact she will probably be a keen dancer herself, She will love children and animals, although not necessarily in that order, and she will make a good, if somewhat authoritarian, mother.

2) Should you be a woman with an ascendant in **Taurus**, your future husband will be of average height, have a strong body with a large chest and well-made legs, and have a tendency to put on weight easily. His face will be broad with large and rather fierce brown eyes, strong featured and quite good-looking. The nose will typically have a plump end to it and be somewhat projecting. The complexion will be darkish and show the marks of early skin ailments, like acne. The hair will be brown, plentiful and curling, yet quite coarse and greasy. He will probably have a lot of body hair. His manner of walking will be a little unusual, tending as he will to sway from side to side, and he may either be slightly bow-legged or suffer from foot problems. Yet he will move quickly and decisively, with a nervous, even tense energy. His sex urge will be strong and demanding. He will be a man of few words, preferring to think before he speaks and to put things concisely. He will not find it easy to discuss personal matters with either you or others. While he will generally be sympathetic and even-tempered, he will be capable of shouting at you, even abusing you verbally, when he gets angry. This is most likely to happen if you make him jealous, which will not be difficult for you to do, so

be cautious in how you behave with other men. He will certainly be contentious and argumentative, and he will need to win any arguments he has with you or with other people. He will enjoy dancing and music, and he may have some musical talents himself. He will tend to do what he wants as he likes to get his own way. Your life with him will be interesting, yet not without its turbulent times and its difficulties.

If you are a man, your wife will probably have an attractive appearance, yet any deficiencies in this regard will be more than compensated for by her strong, almost magnetic personality, of which an important component will be her subtle yet powerful sexuality. Indeed, it is entirely likely that she will make the running in your relationship, for once she has set her sights on anything, whether this be a husband or a job goal, she goes all out to get to it. So be warned that your spouse will be a woman who is driven to succeed and hates to fail. She will certainly push you along, so don't expect much peace if you're not earning top money or if you haven't got the top job. She will probably want to keep on working after marriage, as she will dislike the idea of staying at home doing 'mindless' household chores. She won't even much like the idea of having children, although she will probably compromise on this if you can afford a nanny for them. You will never quite know what she is thinking or feeling, for she needs to keep her inner world hidden to all, so you will have little hope of ever comprehending her underlying motives, although these can perhaps be summed up in one word: power. She is psychologically compelled to dominate and control, and she will use every trick and ploy in the book to keep you and your children firmly under her thumb.

3) If you are a woman with a **Gemini** ascendant, the man you marry will be taller than average, with a long, fleshy, yet striking face, and a body that is strong and well-formed, if somewhat ungainly. He is unlikely, for example, to know quite what to do with his long arms, which he will tend to flap around when he talks. He may have a florid complexion,

which will not be helped by the alcohol and rich food that he loves to consume. Indeed, his indulgence in this respect means that he will probably have trouble with his weight. He may have a prominent nose and large, long, possibly even protruding, teeth, which give him a rather horsey appearance. His hair will be fine and chestnut in colour; he may start to lose it quite early on and be bald in later life. His eyes will be large and clear and somewhat uptilted. He will have a loud, rather booming voice, but he will be a fluent, if not always thoughtful, conversationalist. He will love company and hate being alone, and will thus be drawn to social gatherings of all sorts. Indeed, you and he will have a lot of fun together, although he may be more sports orientated and more of an out-of-door type than you. His weakness, however, is his love of the opposite sex, so you must be prepared for him to flirt and perhaps even be unfaithful to you. This means, as you are not the most faithful type of person yourself, that your marriage will be more threatened in this regard than most others are. Similarly, marital discord may be prompted by his unwillingness to have children, as he does not like to feel tied down and restricted in any way.

Should you be a man, your wife will be an outgoing and rather hearty type, who likes socialising and being involved with others. She will be a good organiser too, which will mean that she will frequently volunteer for, or be asked to take part in, various neighbourhood events and activities, like fêtes and organising raffles. She will be an enthusiastic and energetic home-maker, a good cook, and a fine mother. Indeed, people will frequently wonder how she finds the time for all her various involvements. Yet her hectic pace will be a defence against her two great hates, which are boredom and loneliness. So don't grumble too much when she insists on your presence at yet another whist drive or round on the golf links, as she would soon become bored with your company if she was forced to spend too many evenings at home with you. She will enjoy travel, particularly to exotic places, and she will have a genuine interest in the lives of the people who inhabit them. Yet while her energy and enthusiasm will be very engaging and uplifting at times, notably when you need encouragement, they will be tiring and somewhat overwhelming at others. You will often feel like trying to slow her down and constrain her, yet be careful in this regard as she holds her freedom of movement very dear.

4) Should you be a woman blessed with a **Cancer** ascendant, then the man you marry will probably either be some years older than you are or else you will not marry him until you are quite old. He may even have been married before. He will be shorter than average with a slender, yet wiry physique. His face will be quite long with fine, dry, if somewhat sallow, skin, and large, bright eyes. He will probably have a full head of dark hair, although this may become grey quite early in his life. He may even have a beard. His neck will be long and thin, and he will have a rather narrow chest. Temperamentally, he will be quiet and serious, yet with a sly, subtle and dry sense of humour, and will make you laugh a lot. He will be active, hard working, persevering, and very stoical, seldom ever complaining when things go wrong. However, he may have a tendency to depression. Where money is concerned, he will be very careful, even mean, with it, preferring to save rather than spend it. Because he enjoys exercise and has considerable stamina, he will like walking, particularly in wild and mountainous places, and participating in those sports that are individual, even rather hazardous, in nature. He will have a strong sex drive and may be an accomplished lover, yet he will seldom, if ever, be untrue to you, for he values constancy and faithfulness. Indeed, you and he should enjoy a long, stable and happy union.

If you are a man, your wife will probably be a woman with good looks and a polished, even refined, although perhaps somewhat outspoken, manner. She will certainly try to make the most of her appearance, for she knows the importance of creating a positive impression in any sphere of life, yet she will not have the necessary flair to make the best of herself. In fact there will probably always be something wrong with her clothes (crumpled, stained or out of style, for example), which prevents her from being truly smart. The same applies to her talents as a housewife, which will always be used unevenly and rather haphazardly. She will love artistic display and ethnic design, but not dusting and cleaning, which means that your home could look something like the interior of a Bedouin tent. She will also dislike spending money (saving being her main financial activity), so that the contents of her wardrobe and the furnishings of your home will be purchased mainly from charity shops and from markets. Her security is very precious to her, and she will never do anything to jeopardize it. Hence she will want you to work long and hard and to come home every weekend with the bacon.

5) If you are a woman and your ascendant lies in the zodiac sign of **Leo**, your future (or present) husband will be tall and slim, with colouring that is likely to be dark rather than light. He will have a distinguished, even aristocratic appearance, and his dignity will be very important to him. He certainly will not suffer fools gladly. His face will be long and of even width, with regular and handsome features, and hazel eyes. His forehead will be high, reflecting his superior intelligence, although this will be partly due to the premature recession of his hair; the latter will be fine in texture yet rather greasy. His body will be well-formed and generally strong, but may show prominent veins. It may also be quite hairy. His skin, particularly that of his face, will be smooth and will age well, so that he will have a youthful appearance. He will have an agreeable natural odour, and his clothes will seldom be dirty. While he will be a friendly and generally cheerful type, he will none the less have a serious, thoughtful nature, which will steer him away from all that is shallow, glitzy and self-seeking. He will probably love reading and study, as developing his mind and increasing his knowledge will be very important to him. While he will be fascinated by new inventions and discoveries, he will also have an interest in, and a respect for, the past. He will also have a penchant for anything that is at all odd or unusual. His career will be very important to him and he may devote much of his time to making progress in it, so be

prepared for his single-mindedness in this respect, which may leave you feeling ignored. Because he prizes his freedom, he may prefer to live with you rather than marry you. Yet he will probably be true to you in his fashion.

Should you be a man, your wife will be a slim, energetic and attractive type of woman, although she will not spend too much time worrying about her appearance. She may even have an aversion to wearing make-up or jewellery, and her taste in clothes will be trifle odd, if not eccentric. She will need, for example, to feel comfortable and free and ready for action, which is why she will choose practical, hard-wearing clothes of the type that can be bought from ex-Army stores and from other 'alternative' sources. But in this, as in so many other areas of life, she will be capable of surprising you, as she may enter her boudoir dressed like a navvy and emerge as an elegant princess. She will certainly be an independent type of lady, having a deep love of freedom, which is why she won't appreciate being told what to do or when she's expected to be home. Indeed, she will like going out alone or with friends, often to engage in activities that are probably perfectly innocent, but which she won't want to tell you about. This will take a lot of patience and understanding on your part to deal with, especially as you are a rather jealous type yourself. She will also possess an intelligent and clever mind, one which will always be questioning and probing. She loves to understand how things work, which, combined with her practical bent, means that she will probably be able to mend the car's engine faster and better than you can.

6) If you are a woman with a **Virgo** ascendant, the man you fall in love with and marry will probably be shorter in height than the average, with a rounded, plump body, and a large head. His face will be chubby and pale-complexioned, his eyes large, yet striking and attractive, and brown in colour. His nose will be broad and quite prominent. He will also have fine, thick-growing brown hair. He will move quickly and gracefully, with a sense of purpose and resolve. Yet despite his

efforts to the contrary, he is likely always to look somewhat untidy, his clothes crumpled and stained, and his shoes un-polished and down-at-heel. In fact you will often be irritated by his general untidiness and by his inability to be as regular and as punctual as you are. Despite his determined way of moving, he will lack much inner resolve, tending to be easily discouraged and upset. He may even be prone to bouts of depression, which could lead him to drink more than he ought. However, his manner will be pleasant, easy and sym-pathetic, and he will be very attached to you, to the extent of always trying to do his best by you. He will have good in-tuition, but he will tend to rely on it more than you would wish. He will be quite religious and God-fearing, generous with his time and money and always ready to help someone less fortunate than himself. But because of the underlying ten-sions in your relationship, it is probable that both you and he will marry more than once.

Should you be a man, your wife will probably be on the plump and short side, and she may have thin hair and rather weak teeth. Her complexion may not be much to write home about either. Her dress sense will also be a little unusual, even off-key, and made worse by the fact that her clothes will tend to crumple, stain and snag easily. Because her feet often hurt her, she will be prone to taking her shoes off, often in public places or in other people's homes. She will have difficulty in making up her mind, so when it comes to making decisions, especially the important ones, expect to have to make them all. Yet she will be a very warm, outgoing and friendly type, always ready to help or offer advice to anyone including you. She will have a very good intuitive understanding of others, and it will be second nature to her to spot when she is being lied to or cheated. She will probably also be quite creative, not only as a housewife, but in some artistic capacity, like painting. However, she will be prey to her own imagination, which will at times tip her natural anxiety into actual depres-sion. She will probably have an addictive personality, which means that she will be likely to smoke and drink too much, or even to pop pills when she feels down.

7) If you are a woman with a **Libra** ascendant, your spouse will be an active, impatient and rather pushy sort of person, who likes to get things done now, not tomorrow. He will be of average height or shorter, with a strong and robust, yet hairy body. His face will be rather long, with either a florid or possibly sallow complexion, the eyes round and piercing, the eyebrows dark in colour and thick; they may meet above his nose. He may have a moustache or beard. The hair on his head will be thick, curly and auburn. He may show some form of facial damage, like a scar, or have one or more noticeable moles on his face. He will move quickly and with assurance, for he is a get-up-and-go person, liking uncertainty and adventure. He will not be happy in an ordinary job, especially one that keeps him behind a desk, but will want to be actively engaged in something that keeps him on the move. Because he will be impulsive and somewhat unpredictable, he may change his job suddenly and quite often. He will love the outdoors and new challenges, and he will want to make a success of whatever he does. He will certainly like giving orders. He will also have a quick temper, and he won't want you telling him what to do. Hence, as he will always need to be the boss, you may have to resign yourself to something of a back seat in your relationship. Indeed, he will always put himself first and will regard his needs as more important than your own. If he has some negative influences in his birth chart he may be aggressive, possibly even violent. He will not be entirely honest, for telling lies comes easily to him, and he may have an eye for other women. His sex urge will certainly be strong. Yet your marriage, while it may be marked by rows and shouting, will be different and never dull.

If you are a man, your wife will be an attractive lady with a strong physique, small breasts, and rather more body hair than she would like. She will certainly have a thick, lush crop of hair on her head, which she will need to wash frequently and which she may find hard to style. She will have a good general standard of health, yet will tend to suffer from headaches, hay fever and other head ailments. She will also be prone to feverish complaints. She will be an independent type and will almost certainly want to continue with her career after marriage. Indeed, you may find that she devotes too much time to her job at the expense of her home. She certainly won't be a natural home-maker; not only will she do the housework in fits and starts, but her own untidiness will be a major part of the problem. She will also have a poor money sense, and will often overspend her budget. She will be a chronic impulse buyer, even though she will try to justify herself by claiming she has found some unbeatable bargains. Expect her wardrobe to be stuffed with clothes that she rarely wears. She will be self-centred, irritable, and always late for appointments. However, she will have a strong sex urge and an interest in variety and experimentation, so the nights will be fun even if the days are strained and often argumentative.

8) Should you be a woman with a **Scorpio** ascendant, your future husband will be of average height to taller, with a well-built, somewhat fleshy body, which may become fat in later life. His face will have regular and handsome features, large and beautiful eyes, and, possibly, quite thick lips. His hair will be curly and brown in colour, although it may turn grey quite early. Both his neck and his thighs will be broad and solid-looking, but attractive. His memory will be excellent. He will have a very good appetite, and will enjoy eating and drinking. Indeed, he will like his comforts, being somewhat self-indulgent, and will expect you to be a good cook and entertainer. He will have a generally placid and easy-going personality, and will be well-liked by his wide circle of friends. He will be a hard worker, and both loyal and responsible. While he will prefer you to stay at home and be a conventional wife and mother (he will certainly want to have children), he will be more than happy to provide for you all. He will not be a wanderer, for his interests will be centred on you and the home, and if he does have to travel he will not stay away longer than necessary. He will enjoy country life, gardening, and plants and animals. He will be both attractive to, and attracted by, the opposite sex, and because his sex urge is strong, he may on occasions be tempted into adultery,

although he will normally value your marriage too much to risk being unfaithful.

If you are a man, your wife will probably be a large-boned lady with an ample bosom and a thick neck. Her best facial features will be her large and lustrous eyes, which have a haunting quality to them, and her clear, soft complexion. She may also have a rather husky voice, although it will quickly become strident and rasping when she is angry. She will take some pains with her appearance; she will want to dress well, for example, yet she will seldom look stylish because her conservative tastes and need to get value for money will prevent her from buying anything light, frivolous or up-to-date. Because she will be very much an outdoors type, she will feel most comfortable in hard wearing, practical clothes. Her home is likely to be the centre of her life; she will enjoy doing domestic chores, and entertaining friends and your colleagues will be a pleasure to her. In fact she will simply love it when they express envy or admiration for all that she has, which includes you. This is why she will want her home to be comfortable and well appointed, although when buying for it she will always opt for solidly-made furniture that is somewhat out of fashion. She will probably prefer to start a family quite soon after marriage, as she will love children and the whole idea of motherhood, which will enable her to give up her job and put the tiresome business of forging a career behind her.

9) If you are a woman born with a **Sagittarius** ascendant, the man you settle down with will be of medium height or shorter with a slender, attractive body, long arms and hands, a high, broad forehead, and clear, bright (possibly hazel) eyes. He will be intelligent, talkative, and more interested in the world around him than inner and spiritual matters. He will be curious and investigative, enjoying the company of others and their ideas. And while he may flirt, his unease with intimacy and his low sex-drive will hinder him from having affairs, although he will not be a particularly faithful type. But then neither are you. He will always enjoy the chase more than the consummation. Yet if you can learn to ignore his infidelities,

which are a sign of his underlying immaturity, there is no reason why your marriage should not last. He will be blessed with a great deal of wit and charm, a wide, although somewhat surface knowledge, which he will readily demonstrate in conversation, and, when circumstances call for it, considerable tact and diplomacy. He will not, however, be very dependable, and he will be jealous of his freedom, so do not try to tie him down or restrict him. He will never be entirely happy with married life, nor will he be able to love you as deeply as you would wish, for deep feelings and commitment are foreign to his nature. But if this is understood and he is given the latitude he desires, he will be happy to have you as a permanent anchor in his life.

Should you be a man, your wife will probably be quite tall with a willowy, long-necked body, small breasts, and rather brittle and dry hair. Her complexion will be clear yet rather pale, even pasty, although she could have quite a lot of freckles. Her teeth will be troublesome to her, being small, weak and prone to decay. She will be an active and outgoing type, always full of chatter and ready for a laugh, her manner essentially young at heart and up-to-date. Indeed, she will love anything new and modern and she will be keen to keep up with the latest fashions and styles. She will enjoy the attention of the opposite sex, and she may be an incorrigible flirt, so don't be surprised if she occasionally makes you jealous. In fact your marriage will probably be threatened by outside involvements, especially as you are likely to have an eye for the opposite sex yourself. She will have difficulty in falling in love or in committing herself emotionally to you or anyone; in fact she will distrust her emotions, preferring to run her life by her intellect alone. This means that you can expect to be treated more like a good friend and lover than as a spouse. If you can accept this, then your marriage should be happy and successful, but don't ever try to restrict her in any way. Her independence will be very important to her, and she would rather lose her marriage than lose her freedom. Don't leave her alone, as she will get bored easily – and the Devil finds work for idle hands.

10) If you are a woman and your ascending sign is **Capricorn**, the man with whom you will fall in love and marry will probably be younger than yourself. He may not be very tall, and the upper part of his body will be long compared with the bottom half. His waist will also be quite thick. He will have a roundish face with a straight nose, small eyebrows set on prominent brows, and quite deep-set, light-coloured eyes. The hair and complexion will almost certainly be fair, although a darker colouring is possible. He will have a pleasant, caring and sensitive disposition, and he will be easily hurt and upset. Indeed, he will tend to absorb and reflect the feelings and moods of those around him, which is why it will be important for you to be as positive and optimistic as possible. He will also tend to be somewhat depressive, so that his mood will frequently swing from happy and bright at one moment, to dark and negative at the next. He will enjoy spending time at home and also investing money in it, but while you also enjoy home life, your greater thrift, even meanness, could be a source of tension between you. So might your somewhat sloppy attitude to hygiene and tidiness. He will not be very forceful or ambitious, although with the right sort of urging and encouragement he could achieve far more than he ever thought possible. He will be kind and considerate, always ready to help others and to support charities and good works. In fact he may easily be taken advantage of by the unscrupulous. He will have only a moderately strong sex-drive, certainly one that is less forceful than yours, which could leave you dissatisfied in that respect. Yet there is every reason to suppose that your marriage will be solid, enduring and happy.

Your wife, if you are male, will be a woman of average height and size, with a pale skin and blonde colouring. She may be quite lovely when she is young, yet age won't be all that kind to her, unless she commits herself early on to slowing down its ravages. She will have a tendency to gain weight and to develop wrinkles as she gets older. The latter are one good reason for her not to smoke cigarettes, which aggravate the problem. She will be very warm, tender and loving, and if you treat her as she deserves, she will be a loyal and devoted spouse. She will enjoy being married and running the home, and she probably won't want to continue outside work if your finances are sufficient. However, she will be very practical where money is concerned: she knows its importance and value, and while not at all extravagant, she will work part-time (or even full-time) if necessary to help out with the bills. She will be a very sensitive and intuitive woman, one who is easily hurt by off-hand or thoughtless remarks, so be careful what you say to her. Her ability to assess others will be little short of amazing, for she will have an instinctive understanding of their motives and their honesty. If you listen to what she says in this regard you won't go far wrong. Take warning that she may have depressive tendencies, and that she may, when feeling down, drink too much alcohol.

11) If you are a woman with **Aquarius** as your rising sign, the man you marry or settle down with will be quite tall, with a lithe, strong body, broad shoulders and a dignified bearing and manner. He will have a large, impressive head, an oval face with a pink or ruddy complexion, full bright eyes, and thickly-growing curly hair that may be blonde or reddish in colouring. His way of moving will be lithe and stealthy, and he will characteristically fix his gaze upon anyone he wishes to talk with before approaching them. Indeed, he will give someone his undivided attention when his interest is aroused, yet will completely ignore those who might have upset or ignored him. He will have a pernickity way of eating, and may be a rather fussy and fastidious dresser. He will also be a person of decided views, with whom it is useless to argue. He will be a good organiser, and his natural warmth of manner and friendliness will help him to get on well with his colleagues and associates. He will always need to be in charge, and you may find that you come to resent his rather domineering manner. At work he will be ambitious and loyal, being reluctant to change jobs unless he feels he has been unfairly treated. Indeed, he will have a very acute sense of right and wrong, and will have standards that he will not easily compromise. This quality makes him a stable, responsible partner, which, allied

with his love of his home, means that he will be unlikely to risk his marriage for a brief fling, especially as he considers such an act beneath his dignity. Which means that, as he is also likely to put you on something of a pedestal, you will have every chance of enjoying a long and loving marriage.

Should you be a man, your wife will be a fairly tall, well-built woman, who holds herself erect and who walks and moves quietly, yet with a spring in her step. She will have a thick head of hair, which, if cut simply and well, will be her crowning glory. Her appearance will be very important to her, to the extent that she will rather not go out than exhibit herself in clothes that are creased, worn or out of fashion. She will look particularly stunning in gold jewellery and in anything that is of ethnic origin. Indeed, her looks and her strong personality will gain her a lot of attention, which she will love. This is why you would do well to make her feel that she is the centre of your world, even if that is difficult for you to do. She will be a proud housewife, and she will endeavour to fill her home with smart, stylish and expensive furniture. She will be a good hostess and she will enjoy entertaining, gaining pleasure if her guests exhibit envy at her comforts and her chic. However, she will not want to be only a housewife, so don't expect her to give up her job once you have married. Not only will dusting and cleaning bore her, but she will need to feel in control of her own life and of her finances. She will also have career ambitions that she feels impelled to satisfy. Because she will always want to be in charge, you must anticipate having many struggles with her about who is the boss in your marriage.

12) If you are a woman with a **Pisces** ascendant, the man you marry will be of average height with a slender, light-boned frame, rounded shoulders, and a pleasant, yet probably not particularly good-looking, face. His shy, pale-coloured eyes will be his best feature. He is likely to have brown hair. He will be rather nervous and highly-strung, frequently worried about his health, and something of a hypochondriac. He

will be intelligent and keen on increasing his knowledge; indeed, he will probably have been a bookworm at school. He will like talking and discussing things with you, as he will feel more comfortable in a union based on mental agreement than in one that is primarily physical or emotional. In fact he will have difficulty in dealing with any emotional display. Because he will be an orderly person, who likes everything in its place, he will expect you to be tidy and fastidious about cleanliness, which may mean that many of your disagreements are caused by your failure to live up to his expectations in this regard. Yet he will be witty, engaging and charming, with quite a wide circle of friends and acquaintances. He will always, however, have an eye for the ladies, and he won't think twice before entering into an affair, even though it won't be the extramarital sex he craves but rather the thrill of the chase. He will, in this respect, be immature and selfish. This is why your marriage will frequently be under threat and why you may marry more than once. If you have children there will be more girls than boys, and while he will make sure that they are well provided for, he won't be a particularly warm or doting parent.

If you are a man, your wife will probably be, like you, of average height or less, although physically she will be your opposite, having a slender, even thin body and narrow hips. She will have small breasts. Her best and most beautiful facial feature will be her large, light-coloured eyes, which will draw attention away from her pointed chin and small, rather thin-lipped mouth. She will move quickly and have a general air of impatience, made worse by her high expectations of herself and others. She will take a long time to get ready to go out, taking infinite pains with how she looks; everything she wears will need to be clean, pressed and colour compatible. Yet while she will love looking smart, her somewhat prissy and old-fashioned tastes mean that she will never be entirely up-to-date. She will not be fully at ease with either the world or with you, due to the fact that she is not at ease with herself, for she will distrust her emotions and will be tense about sex. In fact she will be a born worrier, most notably about her

health and about the illnesses (which are often psychoso-
matic) that she may have. Expect her to spend money on
various, often unorthodox, treatments and strange potions.
She will, however, stand by you through thick and thin, mini-
stering to your needs and to those of your children, for she will
have a strong sense of duty. She will love reading and talking,
and will genuinely enjoy domesticity. She may, however,
become an obsessive duster and polisher.

While the zodiac sign on the cusp of your seventh house is
the most important indicator of your present or future spouse's
appearance and character, his or her person and manner may
be somewhat different from that described above if you also
have one or more planets situated in your seventh house,
because it (or they) represent other characteristics possessed
by him. These differences, if any, will also affect the nature of
your marriage and the amount of happiness that it brings you.
Hence if you are already married and find that the above
description linked with your ascending sign does not exactly
fit your spouse, you can be sure that the differences derive
from the planet or planets lying in your seventh house.

Lastly, it is only possible to determine the age at which you
are likely to marry or live with someone by examining your
own birth chart, yet it is worth noting that if you have an
ascendant in Aries, Gemini, Virgo, Libra, Sagittarius or
Pisces, you are more likely to marry at a young age than are
those with the ascendant in a sign other than these.

7

Zodiac Geography

The stars having been solemnly interrogated, Lilly answered,
that the king should retire to the east, into Essex, twenty miles
from London, and Mrs. Whorewood hastened back with this
answer to Hampton Court. Charles, however, had not waited
for it . . .

From the *History of the English Revolution* by F. Guizot

DIFFERENT PLACES have a different effect on all of us. This
applies as much to the houses, shops, and places of entertainment of one's home town, as it does to the town itself and
other urban centres, to particular types of rural landscape, and
to foreign countries. Some people, for example, love city life
and would hate to live anywhere else, while others loathe it
and yearn for the day when they can escape from it. Indeed,
places are very much a case of one man's meat being another
man's poison, and we all recognise how fortunate people are
who find their ideal environment.

Scant research has been done to discover why our tastes
vary so much in this respect. Most of us regard it as a mystery
why one person is attracted, say, to the sea, another to woods
and forests, and yet another to bleak and barren mountains,
each of which seems to cast a magic spell over the person concerned. Such places may not only make us feel relaxed and
happy, but may often also bring us better luck.

The answer to this enigma is provided by astrology, and it is
the purpose of this chapter to name the types of environment
to which you will probably feel most attracted, and those
towns, cities and countries which will be lucky for you. This
information will help you to choose the astrologically best

places in which to live and work, the most fortunate places or countries in which to take a holiday, and, if you are in business, the most propitious districts, towns or countries in which to site your company or sell your goods.

Every type of place, from those in your immediate locality to the immensities of oceans and deserts, is ruled by one or other of the zodiac signs. In general terms, those places most fortunate for you, and most agreeable to you, are ruled a) by your ascending sign, and b) by your Sun sign. You will also feel comfortable in, and possibly benefit from, the places ruled by the signs belonging to the same zodiac triplicity or triplicities.

For example, if your rising sign is Aries, you will be fortunate in the cities, places, and countries that Aries rules, and also, although to a lesser extent, in those governed by Leo and Sagittarius, the other two signs of the Fire triplicity. The same applies to your Sun sign. If your ascendant and the Sun lie in different signs of the same triplicity, then the places ruled by each will be particularly good for you, while if your ascendant and the Sun lie in the same sign, they will cast a highly favourable glow over the places that it rules.

Aries is, in fact, the ruler of mountains and dense forests, upland areas where sheep are pastured; deserts, volcanoes, geysers and hot springs, earthquake zones, meteorite impact sites, caves, and those places where metal ores and gemstones occur. Aries also rules the mines whereby the latter are extracted from the earth. It governs all buildings where fire and/or electricity are used as an energy source, such as kitchens, kilns and blast furnaces, potteries (with Aquarius), iron works, factories, bakeries, crematoria, and power generating stations. The sign is also the ruler of armaments and armouries, and army barracks, parade grounds, military exercise areas, and battlefields, as well as all vehicles used for the deployment of troops, armoured fighting vehicles like tanks, and missile launchers. Similarly, places where cutting tools are made or used, like cutlery manufacturers, machine shops, butchers, slaughter houses, and surgeries, are governed by Aries, as are dye works and chemical factories.

The countries ruled by Aries are England, Germany, Denmark, Iceland, Lithuania, Israel, Syria, Lebanon, Japan, lower Poland and parts of Spain, many of which have a long battle-scarred history, often fighting against each other. No American states are ruled by Aries.

The towns and cities ruled by Aries include Birmingham, Blackburn, Leicester, and Oldham (England); Brunswick (Germany); Utrecht (Holland); Florence, Naples, Padua, and Verona (Italy); Marseilles (France); Krackow (Poland); and Berkeley, Buffalo, Nashville, San Francisco, and Stamford, (United States).

Taurus is the ruler of forests, savannas inhabited by elephants, lakes, exposed rock surfaces, all cultivated farmland (notably fields where cattle are pastured and those in which cereals are grown), and, along with Cancer, rice paddies. It also rules all places where people go to relax and enjoy themselves, such as theatres, cinemas, dance halls, discos, concert halls, public houses, wine bars and amusement arcades, which typically feature music, dance or artistic performance, as well as shops and boutiques where clothes, perfumes, toiletries, flowers, alcoholic drinks, jewellery, musical instruments, gemstones, toys, and sexual appliances are displayed and sold. Taurus similarly rules the factories where such items are manufactured and packaged, and also hotels, guest houses and restaurants; botanical gardens; art galleries and museums; toilets and bedrooms; and brothels and massage parlours.

The countries ruled by Taurus are Ireland, Poland, Azerbaijan, Georgia, Byelorussia (or White Russia) and the Caucasus mountains of Russia, Turkey, Iran, Tasmania and the Mediterranean islands of Cyprus and Rhodes, many of which are predominantly rural and agricultural. The American states of Louisiana, Maryland and Minnesota are also Taurus-ruled.

The towns and cities ruled by Taurus include Ashton-under-Lyne (England); Dublin (Ireland); Leipzig (Germany);

Mantua, Palermo and Parma (Italy); Honolulu (Hawaii); and Oakland, Pittsburgh, and Rochester (NY), (United States).

Gemini, the third sign of the zodiac, has rulership over windy places, reed beds, pebble beaches; trees; the nests and nesting sites of birds, moors and other tracts of land inhabited by game birds, chicken batteries, dove cotes, and turkey and geese farms; limestone quarries; olive groves; and lawns. It is also the ruler of recreation grounds, football stadiums, athletic tracks, basketball, tennis and netball courts, race courses, and sports buildings; all educational establishments like schools, polytechnics and universities; libraries, bookshops, and places where paper and books are manufactured; airports, bus stations, and garages; letterboxes and post offices; radio and television stations; newspaper offices and publishers; factories manufacturing computers, radios, televisions and other communication equipment; trade fairs and trade centres; architects' offices; horse stables; and the residences of authors and poets.

The countries ruled by Gemini are typically small, such as Belgium, Wales, and Armenia, although it also governs the United States, which is one of the largest. Lower Egypt, Lombardy in northern Italy, and the province of Tripoli in Libya, are also under Gemini's jurisdiction, as are the American states of Arkansas, Kentucky, New Hampshire, Rhode Island, South Carolina, Tennessee, and West Virginia.

The towns and cities ruled by Gemini include London, Plymouth, and Wolverhampton (England); Nuremberg (Germany); Versailles (France); Louvain (Belgium); Cordova (Spain); Melbourne (Australia); and Hartford, Houston, Kansas City, Las Vegas, Newport, and Springfield (United States).

Cancer, whose planetary ruler is the Moon, the creator of the tides, is the zodiac sign which governs the sea, river estuaries, streams, canals, lakes (which it jointly rules with Taurus), ponds and reservoirs; islands and promontories, sandy beaches and coastlines in general; dams and aqueducts; flood plains; salt marshes, salt flats, and salt works; wells, water tanks and all water supply systems; coastal and riverside towns and resorts; piers, docks, harbours, and all forms of water transport; swimming pools and bathrooms; gutters and drains; and inland areas where there is high humidity and/or rainfall. Cancer is also the ruler, along with Pisces, of fish restaurants, fish shops, whelk stalls, fish canning factories, and fish farms, maritime suppliers, shops selling fishing tackle; seance rooms; and retailers of predominantly white or pale-coloured objects.

Among the countries ruled by Cancer are Scotland, Holland, Mauritius, New Zealand, Libya, Tunisia, Paraguay, and parts of West Africa, it is also the ruler of the American states of Idaho, Virginia, and Wyoming.

The towns and cities that are ruled by Cancer include York and Manchester (England); St Andrews (Scotland); Amsterdam (Holland); Lubeck (Germany); Berne (Switzerland); Genoa, Milan and Venice (Italy); Cadiz (Spain); Istanbul (Turkey); Tripoli (Libya); Algiers (Algeria); Tunis (Tunisia); and Baton Rouge, Boston, Concord, Niagara Falls, Oklahoma City, Orlando, Richmond, and Santa Fe (United States).

Leo, the fifth sign of the zodiac, presides over thick forests, jungles and savannas which are home to lions and other felines, mountain peaks inhabited by birds of prey, sandy deserts, and hot effusions such as volcanic springs, mud flows, and geysers. As Leo is itself ruled by the Sun, the 'royal' planet, it has governance over all buildings owned yet not lived in by a monarch, also all royal parks, gardens, mazes, lawns, zoos, and crown lands in general; it is likewise the ruler of government buildings, such as the Houses of Parliament and the White House, ministries, embassies and consulates, official residences, town halls and city halls. Forts and fortifications are also ruled by Leo, as are the Bank of England and other banks, money exchanges, cash machines, mints, and gold and diamond mines. Leo governs the places where deck chairs, sun lotions, sun glasses, sun lamps, sun beds, and summer clothing are made and sold. It also has rulership over any inland holiday resort noted for its sunshine. And with Aries, Leo rules over smelters, glass factories, chemical laboratories, and explosives manufacturers.

The countries ruled by Leo are France, Italy, including the Vatican State, Sicily, Romania, Madagascar, the province of Bohemia, and Cappodocia in eastern Turkey. The American states of Alaska, Colorado, Hawaii, Missouri, and New York, are all ruled by Leo.

Among the towns and cities governed by Leo are Bath, Bolton, Blackpool, Bristol, Portsmouth, and Taunton (England); Rome and Ravenna (Italy); Prague (Czechoslovakia); Damascus (Syria); and Albany, Baltimore, Charleston SC, Chicago, Miami, and Rochester (Mn) (United States).

The sign of **Virgo**, whose ruling planet, like Gemini, is Mercury, has rulership over pampas, prairies and other grassy plains, meadows and downland, corn fields, peat bogs, and the surface of the ocean. In the city it governs institutions of mathematics, science and literature; firms of accountants, stockbrokers and stock exchanges; postage stamp printers and stamp collections; messenger services; buildings occupied by MI5, the CIA and other secret services; chemical plants; nursery schools and playgrounds; bingo halls and shooting galleries; health spas, cosmetic surgeries, and places manufacturing laxatives, enemas, anti-haemorrhoid lotions, antiseptics and nerve tonics; places where rope, twine, brooms and brushes, domestic cleansers, animal traps and bird cages are made; and taxidermists and hardware stores.

The countries ruled by Virgo are Switzerland, Turkey, Iraq, Brazil, the West Indies, the Congo and Zimbabwe, Crete and the Peloponnese of Greece, Croatia in the former Yugoslavia, and the Silesia region of Poland and Czechoslovakia. The American state of California is also ruled by Virgo.

The towns and cities ruled by Virgo include Bury, Cheltenham, Maidstone, Norwich and Reading (England); Navarre, Lyons and Paris (France); Basle (Switzerland); Heidelberg (Germany); Padua (Italy); Baghdad (Iraq); Jerusalem (Israel);

Moscow (Russia); and Colorado Springs and Los Angeles (United States).

Libra, the seventh sign of the zodiac, rules over those forests, grasslands and corn fields set at a high altitude, the nesting sites of sparrows and doves, and all roads, lanes, tracks, and footpaths. Sugar plantations, groves where bananas are cultivated, and orchards where peaches, apricots and other exotic fruits are grown are also ruled by Libra. The sign governs factories where sweets and chocolates are made, beehives and the bottling of honey, sugar packers, and the counters or shops where such products are sold. It has jurisdiction over all marriage bureaux, dating agencies, escort services, places where civil marriages are performed, honeymoon suites and resorts, sex shops, parks and buildings frequented by prostitutes, the manufacturers of pillows, bed linen, and luxury goods in general. And being the sign of the Balance, Libra rules all places where people or articles are weighed, and those, like Weight Watchers' gyms, where weight is lost.

The countries ruled by Libra are Austria, Argentina, China, Tibet, Burma, upper Egypt, the department of Savoy in France, Siberia in Russia, and certain Pacific islands. No American state is ruled by Libra.

Included among the towns and cities ruled by Libra are Leeds (England); Vienna (Austria); Copenhagen (Denmark); Antwerp (Holland); Frankfurt am Main, Frieburg and Speyer (Germany); Lisbon (Portugal); Johannesburg (South Africa); and Eugene, Rapid City, Knoxville, Waco and Alexandria (United States).

Scorpio, the eighth sign of the zodiac, has Mars as its traditional planetary ruler, although its secondary ruler is Pluto. The latter's influence accounts for its rulership of openings in the earth, which are dark and forbidding, like caverns, gullies and crevices, of hidden places, and of deserts and related areas where scorpions live, and/or poisonous snakes and other reptiles, or where ant-hills and molehills are found. Similarly, Scorpio has governance over dens, strong rooms, safes, vaults, secret cupboards and recesses, labyrinths, catacombs, dark rooms, mortuaries, funeral homes, graveyards, cemeteries and cenotaphs. It is also said to rule paths and trackways across steep and dangerous mountains and through dense jungle. Mars gives Scorpio rulership over kitchens, bakeries, crematoria, places where funeral pyres are burned, and fortifications like trenches, which have been dug, or those created with barbed wire.

The countries or areas presided over by Scorpio are Norway, Algeria, Morocco, Korea, the Jutland peninsula, Bavaria in Germany, the province of Transvaal in South Africa, and the province of Catalonia in Spain. The American states of Montana, Nevada, North Carolina, North Dakota, Oklahoma, South Dakota, and Washington, are likewise ruled by Scorpio.

The towns and cities governed by Scorpio include Dover, Hull, Liverpool, Newcastle, Stockport and Worthing (England); Ghent (Belgium); Messina (Sicily); Fez (Morocco); and Decatur, Denver, Fresno, Jefferson City, Little Rock, Newark, Philadelphia, St Louis, St Paul, and West Palm Beach (United States).

Sagittarius, ruled by the planet Jupiter, which is named after the king of the gods, has governance over all royal palaces where the monarch actually resides, such as Buckingham Palace, and over those religious centres, like Westminster Abbey, where he or she is crowned. It also rules ancient stone circles that were constructed for religious purposes, and places where religious sacrifices are performed. Law courts and legal offices, military camps, stores and canteens, ammunition depots and infantry divisions are ruled by Sagittarius, as are all cavalry regiments, stables, race courses, gymkhanas and betting shops, travel agents, treasuries, and furniture manufacturers and retailers. The sign also rules outdoor areas that are inhabited by herds of wild horses.

The countries or areas governed by Sagittarius are Spain, Hungary, Saudi Arabia, Chile, Pakistan, Australia, Dalmatia and Slovenia in former Yugoslavia, the province of Moravia in Czechoslovakia, the Tuscany region of Italy, and Provence in France. The sign also rules the American states of Delaware, Illinois, Indiana, Mississippi, New Jersey, and Pennsylvania.

Sagittarius-ruled towns and cities include Nottingham, Sheffield, Sunderland and West Bromwich (England); Rotterdam (Holland); Avignon and Narbonne (France); Cologne (Germany); Naples (Italy); Toledo (Spain); Buda (Hungary); and Anchorage, Cheyenne, Columbia, Columbus GA, Long Beach, Memphis, San Diego, San Jose, Spokane, Tampa and Wilmington (United States).

Capricorn, the sign of the Goat, has rulership, perhaps not surprisingly, over mountainous and rocky places, notably those which experience heavy rainfall and/or give rise to rivers. Indeed, rivers and their banks, and fresh-water marshes, are also ruled by Capricorn, as are the forests growing on mountain slopes. Places of work are generally governed by Capricorn, as are all council and administrative offices; farms, especially those devoted to sheep and goats; uncultivated farmland; ruins; athletic grounds, centres for the homeless; temple precincts; tombs and churchyards; buried hoards of treasure; hermitages and religious retreats; building sites; mines; servants' quarters; bedrooms (with Taurus), and all places that manufacture or sell beds.

The countries and areas ruled by Capricorn are often mountainous or have extensive mountain ranges, namely Albania, Bulgaria, Lithuania, Macedonia and Thrace in Greece, Bosnia in the former Yugoslavia, Afghanistan, Mexico, India, Antarctica, the Punjab region of Pakistan, and the provinces of Hessen, Mecklenburg and Saxony in Germany. The American states of Alaska, Connecticut, Georgia, Iowa, New Mexico, Texas, and Utah, are likewise ruled by Capricorn.

113

The towns of Oxford (England); Brussels (Belgium); Brandenburg (Germany); Delhi (India);and Cincinnati, Cleveland, Detroit, New York, Salt Lake City, Seattle, and Tulsa (United States) are all governed by Capricorn.

The planetary ruler of **Aquarius**, like Capricorn, is Saturn, and its co-ruler is Uranus, which explains why the sign governs some disparate places. In the natural world Aquarius is the ruler of all places where water has dried up, which includes those of an essentially permanent nature, such as salt flats, and those which are not, like dry lake and river beds. It is arguable whether or not deserts should be included here, although Aquarius might reasonably be regarded as the co-ruler of deserts along with Aries, Leo and Scorpio. In the world of Man, Aquarius has something of a dual personality, being the ruler of aircraft and aerodromes, aircraft manufacturers, railway stations, the homes of inventors, patent offices, potteries, lead mines and old people's homes, on the one hand, but also of all those places that are grey, grim, dirty, and degenerate, on the other, such as chimneys, gutters, rubbish bins, rubbish dumps, sewage tanks, windy and forsaken places, dens where drunks, criminals or sex perverts gather, borstals, prisons, lunatic asylums, casinos, and the hangouts of prostitutes, pimps and drug addicts. In former times slave plantations were said to be ruled by Aquarius.

The countries and areas governed by the sign are Sweden, Poland, Russia, Abyssinia, the lower Sudan, the Piedmont region of Italy, Prussia and Westphalia in Germany, Tartary in Central Asia, and certain Polynesian islands. The American states of Arizona, Kansas, Massachusetts, Michigan, and Oregon, are also ruled by Aquarius.

Among the towns and cities presided over by Aquarius are Brighton and Stoke-on-Trent (England); Salzburg (Austria); Bremen, Hamburg and Ingoldstadt (Germany); and Dallas, Forth Worth, Galveston, Indianapolis, Milwaukee, New Orleans, Omaha, Salem, Springfield, and Tucson (United States).

Pisces, like Scorpio and Aquarius, has two planetary rulers, namely Jupiter, which it shares with Sagittarius, and Neptune. Through Neptune Pisces has authority, along with Cancer, over the seas and oceans of the world, for while some would give the seas to Cancer and the oceans to Pisces, the division is essentially arbitrary and academic, and certain water courses (see below), while Jupiter imparts to the sign its rulership over all religious sites and their buildings, such as churches, monasteries, temples, mosques and synagogues, the two planets together giving Pisces rulership over holy rivers like the Ganges and their banks. More mundanely, Pisces governs pump houses, water tanks, water purification plants, fish restaurants, marine aquaria (these with Cancer); treasuries; hotels; places where fine furniture and woollens are manufactured and sold; schools of religion and philosophy; charities; and the homes of astrologers and psychics.

The countries and areas ruled by Pisces are Portugal, Calabria in Italy, Normandy in France, Galicia in Spain, the Mediterranean island of Sardinia, Cilicia in Turkey, Samoa, South Asia, Nubia, and, rather inexplicably, the Sahara desert in Africa. The American states of Florida, Maine, Nebraska, Ohio, and Vermont, are also Pisces-ruled.

Lastly, the towns and cities governed by Pisces include Bournemouth, Cowes, Lancaster, Tiverton and Southport (England); Seville (Spain); Regensburg and Worms (Germany); Alexandria (Egypt); and Amarillo, Atlantic City, Laramie, Minneapolis, Phoenix, Reno, Sacramento, and Washington (United States).

But whether or not you are living in the city or the country that is most compatible with you, you can certainly improve your luck when travelling by setting off on the right day and at the most astrologically propitious time.

As we discovered in Chapter One, seven of the primary compass points are linked with one or other of the planets. The four cardinal directions, north, south, east and west, are respectively ruled by Mercury, Mars, the Sun, and Saturn. The direction north-east is governed by Jupiter, north-west by the Moon, south-east by Venus, and south-west, the single exception, by Caput Draconis, which is one of the two nodes of the Moon. Caput Draconis, or the north node, is the point where the Moon crosses the ecliptic when moving into the northern latitude, while Cauda Draconis, or the south node, is the point where the Moon crosses the ecliptic when passing into the southern latitude.

You will find that if you make any journey, for business, relaxation or other reasons, in the direction associated with the planetary ruler of your ascendant or of your Sun sign, then the trip will generally be fortunate for you. Your luck will also be better if you travel when the Moon is waxing. Good fortune will not attend you, however, if you travel when the Moon is waning, particularly if you go in the 'wrong' direction.

Your travel luck can also be either helped or hindered by the day on which you set off. It brings bad luck to travel east on a Saturday or a Monday; west on a Sunday or a Friday; south on a Thursday; and north on a Tuesday or a Wednesday. But you will attract good fortune if you head east on a Tuesday; west on a Wednesday or a Thursday; south on a Monday or a Saturday; and north on a Friday or a Sunday. However, because journeys are rarely made exactly towards one of the cardinal points, you can regard 'north' as that quadrant of the compass between north-west and north-east; 'south' between south-west and south-east; 'east' between north-east and south-east; and 'west' between north-west and south-west.

Thus, for example, a person with a Leo ascendant can expect the best fortune from journeys made to the east, particularly if he sets off on a Tuesday when the Moon is waxing and returns home (i.e. travels west) on, say, the following day, or on another Wednesday, or on the Thursday.

The zodiac signs are also linked with different directions. Some astrologers associate the three Fire signs (Aries, Leo, and Sagittarius) with east, the three Air signs (Gemini, Libra, and Aquarius) with west; the three Earth signs (Taurus, Virgo, and Capricorn) with south; and the three Water signs

(Cancer, Scorpio, and Pisces) with north. Again, the direction in question can be taken as referring to the quadrant mentioned above. Others, however, say that the direction east is ruled solely by Aries, while Leo and Sagittarius rule jointly over the south-east. And similarly, they regard the west as belonging to Gemini and the north-west to Libra and Aquarius; the direction south to Taurus and the south-west to Virgo and Capricorn; and the north to Cancer and the north-east to Scorpio and Pisces.

Unfortunately the compass directions linked with the zodiac signs do not accord with those given to the planets and so it is difficult to account for the rationale behind them. However, it is said that you can gain good fortune by travelling in the direction associated with your ascending sign or from that occupied by the Moon at the time you depart. But as mentioned before, make sure that the Moon is waxing and that you leave on a propitious day of the week.

8

Luck and the Signs

The way of fortune is like the Milky Way in the sky; which is a meeting or knot of a number of small stars, not seen asunder, but giving light together. So are there a number of little and scarce discerned virtues, or rather faculties and customs, that make men fortunate.

From *Of Fortune* by Francis Bacon

I F YOU are like most people you probably wish that your luck was better. You might even believe that you're not a lucky person at all, that you always seem to miss out on the breaks, that you are never in the right places at the right time, and that Fortune generally tends to look the other way when you're around.

But if that's true there must be a reason for your bad luck, for Fortune, like Cupid, is blind. This means that your luck can probably be improved. Indeed, it is the purpose of this chapter to show you how to attract good luck with the same readiness that nectar attracts bees.

Lucky Days

Luck often results from astrological harmony, which happens, for instance, on the day of the week when the planetary ruler of the day is the same as that of your Sun sign. Such a day will tend to be luckier than most for you. Sunday, for example, which is ruled by the Sun, is most fortunate for Leos, just as Moon-ruled Monday is luckiest for Cancers, Mars-ruled Tuesday is for Arians and Scorpios, Mercury-ruled Wednesday is for Geminis and Virgos, Jupiter-ruled Thursday is for Sagittarians and Pisceans, Venus-ruled Friday is for Taureans and Libras, and Saturn-ruled Saturday is for Capricorns and Aquarians. This means that if you can arrange to go for that important job interview, take your driving test, date a new person whom you want to impress, or do anything that requires some extra luck, on your astrologically most fortunate day, then you can expect to benefit accordingly.

From one to three days of the week, however, are in disharmony with, and so unlucky for, almost all of the zodiac sign types. Arians and Scorpios, for instance, have one unlucky day, which is Wednesday, while Taureans and Libras have two, namely Monday and Sunday. Monday is the single unlucky day for Geminis and Virgos, just as Friday and Saturday are unlucky for Leos. Those born under Sagittarius and Pisces also have two unlucky days, Wednesday and Friday, while poor Capricorns and Aquarians have three, Sunday, Monday and Tuesday. Cancerians by contrast, are the most fortunate in this respect, as none of the days of the week are specifically unlucky for them. The remaining days of the week are of course astrologically neutral as far as luck is concerned.

Lucky Hours

To get the very best of your lucky day, make use, where possible, of your lucky planetary hours. These are the hours ruled by your planetary ruler. They are also the most fortunate hours for you on other days of the week.

If you were born under Cancer, for example, the hours ruled by the Moon are luckiest for you, just as those ruled by the Sun are luckiest for Leos, by Mars for Arians and Scorpios, by Mercury for Geminis and Virgos, by Jupiter for Sagittarians and Pisceans, by Venus for Taureans and Libras, and by Saturn for Capricorns and Aquarians.

The planetary hours of a day always follow one another in the same order, which is: the Sun, Venus, Mercury, the Moon, Saturn, Jupiter, and Mars, after which the sequence is repeated. However, on any particular day, the sequence always starts at sunrise with the planetary hour having the same ruler as the day itself. Thus on a Wednesday, for example, being ruled by Mercury, the first hour is the hour of Mercury, the next of the Moon, the next of Saturn, then of Jupiter, of Mars, of the Sun, and of Venus, after which the sequence starts again with another hour of Mercury.

The time the sun rises varies throughout the year, which is why your lucky hours will constantly shift, not only on your own lucky day, but on any of the other days of the week. But as many newspapers give the sunrise time, it is not hard to work out when your lucky hours will occur.

Let us consider a Wednesday in, say, November when the sun in Great Britain rises at 7.15 a.m. The first hour, that is, 7.15 to 8.15 a.m. will belong to Mercury and will therefore be particularly fortunate for all Geminis and Virgos, although its early time makes it difficult to put it to good use. But if we then count on six hours to 2.15 p.m., we come to the start of the next hour of Mercury that day, which lasts until 3.15 p.m. This will naturally be the best hour of the day to schedule events that require all the luck you can get.

The following table gives the planetary hour sequence for each weekday starting at sunrise. After the 7th hour the sequence repeats itself until sunset.

Sunrise	Sunday	Monday	Tuesday	Wednesday	Thursday	Friday	Saturday
1st hour	Sun	Moon	Mars	Mercury	Jupiter	Venus	Saturn
2nd	Venus	Saturn	Sun	Moon	Mars	Mercury	Jupiter
3rd	Mercury	Jupiter	Venus	Saturn	Sun	Moon	Mars
4th	Moon	Mars	Mercury	Jupiter	Venus	Saturn	Sun
5th	Saturn	Sun	Moon	Mars	Mercury	Jupiter	Venus
6th	Jupiter	Venus	Saturn	Sun	Moon	Mars	Mercury
7th	Mars	Mercury	Jupiter	Venus	Saturn	Sun	Moon

At sunset (see table overleaf) the day sequence is interrupted and the first hour of the evening is ruled by the planet

Sunrise	Sunday	Monday	Tuesday	Wednesday	Thursday	Friday	Saturday
1st hour	Jupiter	Venus	Saturn	Sun	Moon	Mars	Mercury
2nd	Mars	Mercury	Jupiter	Venus	Saturn	Sun	Moon
3rd	Sun	Moon	Mars	Mercury	Jupiter	Venus	Saturn
4th	Venus	Saturn	Sun	Moon	Mars	Mercury	Jupiter
5th	Mercury	Jupiter	Venus	Saturn	Sun	Moon	Mars
6th	Moon	Mars	Mercury	Jupiter	Venus	Saturn	Sun
7th	Saturn	Sun	Moon	Mars	Mercury	Jupiter	Venus

lying sixth from the day's own ruler, *which is counted as the first planet.* Thereafter the same sequence is followed, which runs through the night until sunrise of the next day. Thus on Thursday, for example, which is ruled by Jupiter, the first hour after sunset is ruled by the Moon, the next by Saturn, the next by Jupiter, the next by Mars, the next by the Sun, the next by Venus, and the next by Mercury, after which the sequence repeats itself. The table above shows the planetary sequence of hours as it applies to each night of the week.

Thus the luckiest night hours for Arians and Scorpios on a Tuesday when the sun sets at, say, 6.35 p.m. will be between 8.35 and 9.35 p.m. (the first hour of Mars) and 3.35 to 4.35 a.m. (the second hour of Mars). They will have, as will each sign type, lucky hours at different times on different nights of the week, which can be found by referring to the table shown above.

Lucky Gemstones

The twelve signs of the zodiac each have a number of gemstones that are potentially lucky when worn by those born under the sign or who have it rising at their birth. Ideally, the gemstone should touch the skin, which it will if it forms part of an open-backed ring or is worn as a pendant. If you wish, you can test the efficacy of your preferred birth stone (chosen from among those which are potentially lucky for your sign) by tying it to your left arm with a piece of silk ribbon the same colour as the stone. Leave it in place for three days. If during this time your luck improves, you can wear the stone from then on with confidence. Should your luck worsen, however, remove the stone immediately, and test the others in turn until you find one that gives you a good result.

Tradition assigns a principal or primary gem plus a number of secondary stones to each zodiac sign shown below. Wear the primary stone if possible, but if it is too expensive – or if it fails the test mentioned above – then choose one of the secondary stones. These gems will not only improve your luck but will also bring you a number of other benefits, which I describe for each of the primary stones. However, if you have, say, a health complaint for which one particular stone is the remedy, then don't hesitate to wear the stone even though it might not be assigned to your zodiac sign. It will still benefit your health even though it might not improve your luck.

Zodiac sign	Primary stone	Secondary stones
Aries	diamond	ruby, bloodstone
Taurus	emerald	moss agate, lapis lazuli
Gemini	agate	opal, onyx, alexandrite
Cancer	ruby	turquoise, moonstone, pearl, emerald
Leo	sardonyx	topaz, diamond, peridot
Virgo	sapphire	cornelian, diamond, chrysolite
Libra	opal	aquamarine, jade, chrysolite
Scorpio	topaz	ruby, beryl, cornelian, malachite
Sagittarius	turquoise	sapphire, zircon, carbuncle
Capricorn	garnet	black opal, tourmaline
Aquarius	amethyst	lapis lazuli, aquamarine
Pisces	bloodstone	sapphire, pearl, coral, moonstone

She who from April dates her years,
Diamond shall wear, lest bitter tears
For vain repentance flow; this stone,
Emblem for innocence is known.

The *diamond*, made of pure carbon crystallised under enormous pressure, is the hardest naturally occurring substance and shines with a bright sparkle, which is why it is the most expensive and most sought after gemstone. In ancient times it was believed to confer courage, frighten away ghosts and wild beasts, and give victory over one's enemies. The curative action of the diamond is well-suited to Arians as it has its greatest effect on the head and brain, and it will stop headaches, ease depression, prevent nightmares, and even cure insanity when worn, preferably on the left side of the body. It is also said to protect the wearer from injury during riots and from bewitchment.

> Who first beholds the light of day,
> In spring's sweet flowery month of May,
> And wears an Emerald all her life,
> Shall be a loved, and happy wife.

The *emerald* is composed of crystallised silica, aluminium oxide, and glucinum, mixed with traces of iron and chromium. Its cool green colour is believed to originate from an oxide of the latter element, namely chromium sesqui-oxide. The stone has a variety of curative properties, of which the most important is its ability to restore poor eyesight and combat eye ailments. It is also said to stop bleeding (when placed in the mouth), ease childbirth, and cure epilepsy, dysentery, and the plague. Modern Taureans might find its ability to cure phobias and other psychological fears particularly useful.

> Who comes with summer to this earth,
> And owes to June her hour of birth,
> With ring of Agate on her hand,
> Can health, wealth, and long life command.

The *agate* is a variety of silicon dioxide or quartz mixed with oxides of iron. It takes its name from the Achates river in Sicily, where legend says that the gems were first found. They were thereafter highly prized by the Romans, notably for their ability to neutralize snake bites when finely ground into water and drunk. The agate is well-known for its power to promote fertility, and in former times farmers and gardeners would tie an agate to their left arm when tending their crops, in the belief that it would increase their yield. The stone will of course bring good fortune to the Gemini-born when worn by them.

> The glowing Ruby shall adorn
> Those who in warm July are born;
> Then will they be exempt and free
> From love's doubt, and anxiety.

The *ruby* is a crystalline form of aluminium oxide and magnesium oxide, and its name derives from the Latin *rubus* meaning 'red'. The gem is reputed to darken in colour when its wearer has been poisoned or is about to suffer harm, although its ability to lift the spirits and encourage cheerfulness is perhaps its most useful property today. The ruby thus banishes despondency, calms the mind, and, or so it is said, prevents nightmares. Those who are suffering from an over-active libido should wear the ruby, for it calms the passions, and those who spend too freely, will find it helpful also for the ruby has a reputation for stimulating thrift and good sense.

> Wear Sardonyx, or for thee
> No conjugal felicity;
> The August-born without this stone,
> 'Tis said, must live unloved, and lone.

The *sardonyx* is a variety of onyx which reputedly takes its name from the ancient Persian capital of Sardis. Chemically it is a form of amethyst or quartz containing chalcedony, the latter being responsible for its characteristic flesh-coloured sheen. In addition to improving the luck of its wearer, sardonyx will, like the ruby, combat depression and lift the spirits.

Formerly it was worn to cure or prevent epileptic fits, and when inscribed with the outline of a quail and a sea tench was said to make the wearer invisible, although I have not been able to personally verify this surprising property!

> A maiden born when autumn leaves
> Are rustling in September's breeze,
> A Sapphire on her brow should bind;
> 'Twill cure diseases of the mind.

The lovely blue *sapphire* is the hardest gemstone after the diamond, although it chiefly consists of crystalline aluminium oxide mixed with traces of iron oxide and cobalt. The principal medical property of the sapphire is its reputed ability to cure eye ailments, including blindness, when held against the eyes; it will likewise stop nosebleeds when placed on the forehead. When worn, it is said to heal soreness, ulcers, and, remarkably enough, haemorrhoids. Other useful properties of the sapphire include protecting the wearer from his or her enemies and from enchantment.

> October's child is born for woe,
> And life's vicissitudes must know;
> But lay an Opal on her breast,
> And hope will lull those foes to rest.

The *opal* is a form of amorphous quartz, being made from compressed hydrated silica jelly, and like both the sardonyx and the bloodstone it was believed to render its wearer invisible; however, this did not mean that the person actually vanished but that the eyes of others were directed away so that the wearer was simply not seen. The opal is regarded as being generally good for the health, and specifically it is said to cure eye ailments. It also has a beneficial influence on the mind, calming both the thoughts and enlivening the senses, and it is sometimes worn to turn another's liking into love.

> Who first comes to this world below,
> With drear November's fog, and snow,
> Should prize the Topaz's amber hue,
> Emblem of friends, and lovers true.

The *topaz* is a rock crystal consisting of silicon dioxide, aluminium oxide and fluoride. Its colour is extremely variable. Its name derives from the legendary Red Sea island of Tapazion, where the gems were first discovered. When worn on the left arm or as a pendant, the topaz will reputedly give courage, banish fear of the dark, calm the temper, and cure madness. The stone responds to the waxing Moon by becoming more effective, while it loses its strength when the Moon wanes. It will also protect against witchcraft and sorcery, and it is said to stop bleeding.

> If cold December gives you birth,
> The month of snow, and ice, and mirth,
> Place on your hand a Turquoise blue;
> Success will bless whate'er you do.

Chemically the *turquoise* consists of hydrated phosphate of aluminium mixed with cupric oxide, of which the last is responsible for the gem's beautiful blue or blue-green colour. However, the colour of the turquoise varies in response to the wearer's physical state, becoming paler if he or she sickens. It is also unusual, it is said, in protecting the wearer from the effects of a fall from whatever height, although I have not personally checked out this assertion. Like several of the stones already mentioned the turquoise will improve the sight and uplift the spirits; it will also bring good fortune if it is received as a gift, but not if it is bought. Horse-riding readers will be interested to learn that the stone, when worn, will protect them against being thrown or injured by their mounts.

> By her in January born
> No gem save Garnets should be worn;

> They will ensure her constancy,
> True friendship, and fidelity.

The *garnet*, a stone of variable colour, has a composition similar to that of the ruby. In addition to the benefits described in the above verse, the garnet, like the ruby, will banish depression and generally improve the mood, and will also reportedly, when tied with cloth to the forehead, allow the wearer to see in the dark. If held in the mouth the gem will dissolve away tartar from the teeth. The garnet is also said to prevent wounding and injury, heart disease, and stem the spitting of blood from the mouth.

> The February-born shall find
> Sincerity and peace of mind,
> Freedom from passion and from care,
> If they the Amethyst will wear.

The *amethyst* gets its name from the Greek word *ametho* meaning 'sobriety', which indicates that the stone was originally used as a specific against drunkenness. The gem is a variety of quartz, its unique colour deriving from the manganese oxide it contains. It is said to be most effective in bringing good fortune and its other benefits when it is tied or taped to the navel. The benefits of amethyst are many, for, in addition to preventing drunkenness, the stone will help keep the brain alert and active, stop evil or lecherous thoughts, impart wisdom and understanding, reduce the amount of sleep needed, protect against injury, and give skill in business. Indeed, you won't go far wrong if you wear one of these beautiful and inexpensive gems.

> Who in this world of ours, her eyes
> In March first opens, shall be wise.
> In days of peril, firm and brave,
> And wear a Bloodstone to her grave.

The *bloodstone* or heliotrope is a type of jasper, green in colour yet speckled with red reminiscent of blood splatters, which derive, or so legend has it, from the blood of the crucified Christ, hence the gem's name. In turn, by vibrational reciprocity, the bloodstone is said to be highly effective in staunching bleeding when held against a wound. When worn as described it imparts wisdom and makes the wearer constant and reliable, brings fame and fortune, and prolongs the life. Few other stones can confer such wonderful benefits.

It is usual for the above mentioned gemstones to be set in either gold or silver. These metals should certainly be worn by the Leo-born (gold) and the Cancer-born (silver), with or without gemstones, because they are lucky for them. The other lucky zodiac sign metals are as follows, and should be worn or carried, if possible, by those born under them: iron (Aries and Scorpio), copper (Taurus and Libra), quicksilver (Gemini and Virgo), tin (Sagittarius and Pisces), and lead (Capricorn and Aquarius). The problem metal here is quicksilver or mercury, which is not only difficult to obtain, but is tricky to wear or carry about, being a liquid at room temperature. It is also poisonous. However, because it is commonly used in thermometers to register the rise and fall of the temperature, you can, if born under Gemini or Virgo, improve your luck by carrying a medical thermometer around with you (which Virgos should feel happy doing) and by hanging a thermometer in your home. Lead too is poisonous so would be best kept in a small phial.

Lucky Colours

As with gemstones, each sign of the zodiac has a number of colours that are lucky for those born under it, or who have it rising at the moment of their birth. Of these, one is the principal colour, and the remainder are secondary colours. Yet while the primary colour is the most powerful and fortunate, each colour is lucky for the sign type in question. Because all the colours have a particular personality dimension, you will probably find that either the primary colour or one of the secondary colours of your birth sign or rising sign is your favourite colour.

To bring yourself luck and to bring out the best in yourself, you should ideally always wear one or other of your astrological colours. This does not mean that your whole outfit has to be that colour; indeed, it is often best simply to wear a shirt or a blouse (or a pullover or cardigan) of that colour, these being garments that cover the heart and chest and which are not normally removed (as a jacket may be) during the day. Because each zodiac sign is associated with at least three colours, and because you may well have a different rising sign from your Sun sign, you will have six or more colours to choose from for your wardrobe. As these can be mixed together, or even with other colours, you should find that you have plenty of variety.

You do not have to limit your lucky colours to your clothes. You can choose a car sprayed with one of them, or employ them in your home decorations and furnishings, or even have a pet that has fur or feathers of that colour.

The lucky colours of each zodiac sign are shown below:

Zodiac sign	Principal colour	Secondary colours
Aries	red	pink, yellow
Taurus	green	orange, indigo, blue
Gemini	yellow	orange, light green
Cancer	white	amber, emerald green
Leo	gold	yellow, orange
Virgo	yellow	pale blue, jade green
Libra	green	blue, violet
Scorpio	red	russet, brown, blue
Sagittarius	purple	orange, blue, mauve
Capricorn	black	indigo, grey
Aquarius	violet	electric blue/green
Pisces	blue	purple, mauve, sea green

Lucky Numbers

Your zodiac sign has one or two single numbers that are lucky for you. Double or larger numbers will also be lucky for you if they reduce as described. For example, supposing your lucky number is 4 and that your house number is 58. Is the latter a lucky number for your? To find out first add the 5 and the 8 together:

$$5 + 8 = 13$$

Then add 1 and 3 together:

$$1 + 3 = 4$$

As 58 reduces to 4 it is lucky for you, as any large number that reduces to 4 will be also.

The lucky number(s) for Arians and Scorpios is 9; for Taureans and Libras, 6; for Geminis and Virgos, 5; for Cancers, 2 and 7; for Leos, 1 and 4; for Sagittarians and Pisceans, 3; and for Capricorns and Aquarians, 8.

The different zodiac sign types have certain zodiac periods of the year which are either lucky or unlucky for them. You

Zodiac sign	Lucky periods	Unlucky periods
Aries	Cancer, Leo	Scorpio, Pisces
Taurus	Gemini, Cancer, Sagittarius	Libra, Scorpio
Gemini	Libra, Capricorn, Aquarius	Pisces
Cancer	Libra, Capricorn	Gemini, Aquarius
Leo	Leo, Sagittarius, Aquarius	Cancer, Pisces
Virgo	Capricorn, Pisces, Cancer	Aries, Leo, Aquarius
Libra	Capricorn, Pisces	Aries, Virgo
Scorpio	Pisces, Taurus, Virgo	Aries, Gemini, Libra
Sagittarius	Aries, Gemini, Libra	Taurus, Gemini, Scorpio
Capricorn	Taurus, Cancer, Scorpio	Gemini, Leo
Aquarius	Gemini, Leo, Sagittarius	Cancer, Virgo, Capricorn
Pisces	Gemini, Cancer, Libra	Scorpio

can improve your life by using the former to your advantage, by beginning a courtship, marrying, starting a business, taking a vacation, etc., at that time, and by avoiding doing any of these activities during the latter. In fact you should try and keep your head down in your negative zodiac periods, while at the same time being prepared for trouble.

Your own zodiac period is also generally fortunate for you, yet it does not confer the same degree of good fortune as those periods can that are listed as lucky for you above.

9

Zodiac Gardening

I know nobody that possesses more private happiness than you
do in your garden; and, yet no man, who makes his happiness
more public, by a free communication of the art and knowledge of it to others.

From *The Garden* by Abraham Cowley

I F YOU are a keen gardener, you belong to the largest hobby
group in the country, for more than 12 million Britons enjoy
pottering in their flower beds and borders, growing flowers and
shrubs, vegetables and fruit.

Yet despite the fact that people are regularly advised on
how to make their thumbs greener, by gardening experts writ-
ing in magazines and newspapers or pontificating on television, nothing is said by them about the influence of the
planets and the zodiac signs on plant growth, and how, by
paying attention to these astral factors, everyone's garden can
be improved.

Being a gardener myself, I am delighted to be able to tell
you some of the secrets of zodiac gardening. I have no doubt
that if you follow my advice you will soon be rewarded in your
garden by better results attained with less effort.

The Sun is of course the power-house of the garden, providing as it does light and heat, without which nothing at all
would grow. The interaction of both these forms of energy
with the earth's atmosphere gives rise to the weather, which
in turn is modified by the angular inclination and orbital
movement of our planet to produce the seasons. The Sun, in
other words, creates the basic conditions for horticulture and

agriculture, which is why it has always been considered the king among the astrological planets.

The importance of the Sun is an obvious fact of life and every gardener is used to working in step with the weather and the seasons. Less well-known is the influence of the Moon, which is altogether more subtle, shadowy and feminine. For while the Sun is the driving force in your garden, the Moon (and to a lesser extent the remaining planets) is responsible for its fine tuning.

Indeed, the importance of the Moon to plant growth and flowering is recognised in the following nursery rhyme:

> Mary, Mary quite contrary,
> How does your garden grow?
> With silver bells and cockle shells,
> And pretty maids all in a row.

Any bells, but particularly silver bells, are symbols of the Moon, as indeed are cockle shells, whose former inhabitants were marine molluscs. Maidenhood is associated with the New Moon, just as feminine maturity is with the Full Moon and female decrepitude with the Old Moon. And Mary herself, being quite contrary, likewise represents the Moon, which continually undergoes a cycle of growth, from New Moon to Full Moon, and decay, from Full Moon to New Moon. Thus the garden, the rhyme suggests, operates in obedience to the silent and mysterious Moon.

This being the case, if you wish to take full advantage of zodiac gardening lore, you should start by creating the most astrologically harmonious conditions for your plants.

If possible, try to enclose your garden (if it is not already enclosed) with either a brick wall or a wooden fence. A wall is a Sun-ruled, and a fence is a Moon-ruled, boundary that will serve to contain and encourage, in the first case, positive solar influences, and in the second, positive lunar influences, into your garden. These will be further attracted by constructing a circular gate in the wall or fence, whose shape symbolises both planets. One or more round flower beds included in the garden's layout will have the same effect. A privet hedge is also an excellent Moon-ruled boundary for any garden, for although it needs regular clipping in the summer its astrological benefits are well worth the effort. If you plant the golden-leaved variety, so much the better. A pond, particularly one that is circular, will also attract beneficial lunar influences, along with Moon-ruled frogs and toads which will help control slugs, insects and other invertebrate pests. Most water plants are Moon-ruled and so will heighten the lunar resonance of the pond (and garden), and if you add goldfish, being Moon-ruled but also Sun-coloured, they will bring a measure of solar influence to their attractive power.

The Sun should be represented by, and solar forces thus attracted by, a brick-built sundial, around which should be placed Sun-ruled plants like peonies and marigolds. Solar influences are particularly encouraged by the principal Sun-ruled plant, the eponymous sunflower, its height and love of sunshine making it most suitable for a sunny position at the back of a border. Do make sure that the garden is planted with one or more rosemarys, a Sun-ruled shrub, whose fragrant leaves not only symbolise remembrance but can also be used to flavour meat and to make a fine hair tonic. Chamomile, lovage and angelica are three Sun-ruled herbs that can be grown in your herb bed, and the year should be heralded with plenty of saffron crocuses, grown from bulbs, which are also governed by the Sun.

In addition to a pond and a privet hedge, if you have either, beneficial lunar influences can be attracted into your garden by growing Moon-ruled wallflowers, a favourite cottage garden perennial. Irises are also ruled by the Moon, as are white roses, white lilies and most other plants with white flowers, such as candytuft. Grow these in among your other flowering plants and shrubs, and use the smaller species like white alyssum as edgings, for contrast and to promote astrological harmony.

Most sowing or planting out is done during the spring or early summer, and you should of course make sure that you read the instructions on the seed packet or in your gardening book to discover exactly when is the right time for each plant type. Once that has been ascertained, you must then make sure to sow or plant out during the right phase of the Moon, in order to give your seeds or plants the best possible start.

It was mentioned in an earlier chapter that each lunation, that is, the period between one New Moon and the next, lasts twenty nine and a half days. During half of this time the Moon is growing in size or waxing from New to Full, while for the remainder it is decreasing in size or waning. These two periods of lunar change are the keys to good gardening, for each is best for doing different gardening jobs.

The waxing Moon encourages germination, growth, ripening and fruition, thus as a rule of thumb all activities to do with these, such as sowing seeds, transplanting seedlings, potting up, thinning out, grafting, adding fertiliser, and indeed watering, should be done at this time. More specifically, these jobs may be started two days before the New Moon and should continue until three days before the Full Moon.

The waning Moon, by contrast, inhibits germination, retards growth, and generally shrinks and dries. Thus during such a period those jobs mentioned above should be avoided, and the time usefully spent digging, weeding, mowing lawns, deadheading, pruning, controlling pests, etc. Again, such work may be started two days before the Full Moon and carried on until three days before the New Moon.

However, it is important to note that some vegetables do best when planted during the waning Moon. These are the ones whose edible portions develop underneath the ground, such as potatoes, artichokes, carrots, parsnips, swedes, turnips, onions, shallots, and radishes.

Yet all vegetables which produce edible leaves, seeds, fruits or stems, which develop above the ground, like cabbages, lettuces, peas, beans, tomatoes, marrows, melons, celery, endives, rhubarb, and asparagus should be planted when the Moon is waxing. So too should all fruit trees and all flowering bulbs.

This system can be fine-tuned by taking into account the four quarters of the Moon, each of which lasts approximately seven and a half days, the first running from New Moon to

First Quarter (or Half) Moon, the second from First Quarter Moon to Full Moon, the third from Full Moon to Last Quarter Moon, and the fourth from Last Quarter Moon until the Moon vanishes temporarily from the sky. But specifically, the planting periods outlined below may be *started two days before each phase of the Moon and should continue for the following seven days only.*

First Quarter: during this period sow or plant out (or transplant) those vegetables that produce edible leaves, like lettuces, cabbages, brussels sprouts, endives, and spinach, or which have edible stems/leaf petioles, such as celery, leeks, rhubarb, cauliflowers and broccoli.

Second Quarter: this is the best time to sow or plant out (or transplant) those vegetables that have edible fruits, like the tomato, marrow, and cucumber, or which produce enclosed seeds, like the pea, the runner bean, the broad bean, the French bean, etc.

Third Quarter: all vegetables that develop their edible portions underground should ideally be planted during this part of the Moon's cycle.

Fourth Quarter: this is the most unproductive lunar period where planting is concerned, and it is best employed for doing all those other gardening jobs like weeding, digging, cutting the lawn, controlling pests, and deadheading.

The dates on which the Moon reaches its four quarters from the beginning of March to the end of August during the six years from 1994 to 1999 inclusive are given overleaf (N = New Moon; FQ = First Quarter Moon; F = Full Moon; TQ = Third Quarter Moon).

However, if you want to work in full harmony with the Moon, you need to discover which zodiac sign the Moon occupies on that day and adjust your gardening schedule accordingly. The Moon, being the fastest mover of the astrological bodies, passes through all of the zodiac signs (spending approximately two and half days in each of them) during the course of one sidereal month, which lasts 27.3 days, this being

1994	1995	1996	1997	1998	1999
Mar 04 TQ	Mar 01 N	Mar 05 F	Mar 02 TQ	Mar 05 FQ	Mar 02 F
Mar 12 N	Mar 09 FQ	Mar 12 TQ	Mar 09 N	Mar 13 F	Mar 10 TQ
Mar 20 FQ	Mar 17 F	Mar 19 N	Mar 16 FQ	Mar 21 TQ	Mar 17 N
Mar 27 F	Mar 23 TQ	Mar 27 FQ	Mar 24 F	Mar 28 N	Mar 24 FQ
Apr 03 TQ	Mar 31 N	Apr 04 F	Mar 31 TQ	Apr 03 FQ	Mar 31 F
Apr 11 N	Apr 08 FQ	Apr 10 TQ	Apr 07 N	Apr 11 F	Apr 09 TQ
Apr 19 FQ	Apr 15 F	Apr 17 N	Apr 14 FQ	Apr 19 TQ	Apr 16 N
Apr 25 F	Apr 22 TQ	Apr 25 FQ	Apr 22 F	Apr 26 N	Apr 22 FQ
May 02 TQ	Apr 29 N	May 03 F	April 30 TQ	May 03 FQ	Apr 30 F
May 10 N	May 07 FQ	May 10 TQ	May 06 N	May 11 F	May 08 TQ
May 18 FQ	May 14 F	May 17 N	May 14 FQ	May 19 TQ	May 15 N
May 25 F	May 21 TQ	May 25 FQ	May 22 F	May 25 N	May 22 FQ
Jun 01 TQ	May 29 N	Jun 01 F	May 29 TQ	Jun 02 FQ	May 30 F
Jun 09 N	Jun 06 FQ	Jun 08 TQ	Jun 05 N	Jun 10 F	Jun 07 TQ
Jun 16 FQ	Jun 13 F	Jun 16 N	Jun 13 FQ	Jun 17 TQ	Jun 13 N
Jun 23 F	June 19 TQ	Jun 24 FQ	Jun 20 F	Jun 24 N	Jun 20 FQ
Jun 30 TQ	Jun 28 N	Jul 01 F	Jun 27 TQ	Jul 01 FQ	Jun 28 F
Jul 08 N	Jul 05 FQ	Jul 07 TQ	Jul 05 N	Jul 09 F	Jul 06 TQ
Jul 16 FQ	Jul 12 F	Jul 15 N	Jul 12 FQ	Jul 16 TQ	Jul 13 N
Jul 22 F	Jul 19 TQ	Jul 23 FQ	Jul 20 F	Jul 23 N	Jul 20 FQ
Jul 30 TQ	Jul 27 N	Jul 30 F	Jul 26 TQ	Jul 31 FQ	Jul 28 F
Aug 07 N	Aug 04 FQ	Aug 06 TQ	Aug 03 N	Aug 08 F	Aug 04 TQ
Aug 14 FQ	Aug 10 F	Aug 14 N	Aug 11 FQ	Aug 14 TQ	Aug 11 N
Aug 21 F	Aug 18 TQ	Aug 22 FQ	Aug 18 F	Aug 22 N	Aug 19 FQ
Aug 29 TQ	Aug 26 N	Aug 28 F	Aug 25 TQ	Aug 30 FQ	Aug 26 F

the time it takes for the Moon to return to the same point in the sky. Because the synodic month (between one New Moon and the next) is longer than the sidereal month, this results in the New Moon (or any other phase of the Moon) invariably occupying the next zodiac sign to the one it did previously. The Moon's zodiac position on any day can be found by consulting an ephemeris.

Such adjustment of your schedule is necessary to take into account the influence, for better or worse, of the zodiac signs on the Moon. For some zodiac signs enhance the Moon's effects in the garden, while others retard them. The former are the signs belonging to the Water triplicity (Cancer, Scorpio, and Pisces) and to the Earth triplicity (Taurus, Virgo, and Capricorn), which is why they are known as the *fruitful* signs. The latter are the signs belonging to the Fire triplicity (Aries, Leo, and Sagittarius) and to the Air triplicity (Gemini, Libra, and Aquarius), which is why they are called the *barren* signs.

Thus in order to get the very best results from your gardening, with regard to the number of seeds germinating, the most vigorous and healthy growth of your seedlings and older plants, and the maximum number of fine flowers and fruits, you should sow, pot up, plant out, transplant, take cuttings, layer, bud and graft, and generally care for your plants, when the Moon is not only waxing but is located in one or other of the fruitful signs.

The Moon will, of course, often pass through a barren sign when it is waxing. Such a placement does not entirely negate the Moon's beneficial influence, but it does lessen it. Where possible, do not sow or plant out at this time but use such periods for jobs like mulching, fertilising, earthing up potatoes, putting in pea sticks, turning the compost heap, clipping hedges, and cutting lawns. But flowering bulbs may be planted now.

When the Moon is waning but inhabiting a fruitful sign, spend your time doing those garden tasks that are largely preparatory, such as digging, hoeing, placing nets over fruit bushes and ponds, laying paths, building rockeries, and raking leaves, but also take advantage of the fact that this is the ideal period for planting out those vegetables with edible roots or tubers, like carrots, potatoes, artichokes, and radishes. Fruit trees can also be pruned with advantage now.

Lastly, when the Moon is waning, particularly when it is in its Last Quarter, and is placed in a barren sign, your gardening jobs should be of the destructive type. Burn leaves and other garden wastes, weed beds and paths, spray insects, put down slug pellets, etc.

If you wish to encourage the grass of your lawn to grow more quickly, then cut it during the First and Second Quarter of the

Moon when she is located in a fruitful sign. Conversely, if you want to slow the growth of your lawn, cut it when the Moon is waning yet lodged in a fruitful sign. Be warned that if you cut your lawn when the Moon is both waning and sited in a barren sign, you may find that the grass will not only grow slowly, but poorly too, which may lead to the development of bare patches. These lunar effects also apply to the clipping of hedges.

The choice of vegetables and fruit you grow in your garden should be dictated by your Sun sign's ruling planet and by those of the other two signs belonging to its triplicity. Your rising sign's planetary ruler, if different, is also relevant. This is because, as I explained in Chapter 2, these will be the foods best suited to your body and its dietary needs. The list below gives the planetary ruler of each of the commonest vegetables, fruits, and herbs, and will enable you to plan easily what to grow:

The Sun (rules Leo): angelica, apply, bay, lovage, rosemary, rue, saffron, vine

The Moon (rules Cancer): cabbage, cauliflower, celery, cress, cucumber, leek, lettuce, marrow, melon, parsnip*, pumpkin, purslane, shallot, squash, turnip* (* = co-ruled by Jupiter)

Mercury (rules Gemini and Virgo): beans (broad, runner, French, haricot, etc.), caraway, carrot, dill, fennel, fenugreek, horehound, marjoram, mushroom, parsley, pea, savory (summer), savory (winter), valerian

Venus (rules Taurus and Libra): apricot, artichoke, blackberry, cherry, gooseberry, loganberry, mint, peach, pear, pennyroyal, plum, raspberry, strawberry, thyme

Mars (rules Aries and Scorpio): basil, blackcurrant, chives, garlic, horseradish, mustard, onion, rhubarb, red currant, red peppers, spinach, tarragon, tomato

Jupiter (rules Sagittarius and Pisces): asparagus, balm, bilberry, borage, chervil, endive, parsnip*, sage, swede*, turnip* (* = co-ruled by the Moon)

Saturn (rules Capricorn and Aquarius): aubergine, celeriac, chicory, Chilean beet, Jerusalem artichoke, medlar, potato, quince, red beets, salsify, scorzonera, sea-kale beet, sloe, shallot

Where flowers are concerned there are two things to remember. First, you will have most success with those plants that have the same planetary ruler as either your Sun sign or your rising sign, and second, by growing these flowers in your garden it will be in greater astrological harmony with you, thereby bringing you more pleasure, more peace, and more joy.

The list below gives some of the best and most familiar cottage garden flowering plants and shrubs associated with each planet:

The Sun: centaury, chamomile, crocus, eyebright, hyacinth, marigold, peony, pimpernel, rosemary, rue, sunflower

The Moon: candytuft, daffodil, iris, jasmine, narcissus, wallflower, water lily, white alyssum, white rose, winter green

Mercury: azalea, elecampane, honeysuckle, lavender, lily of the valley, scabious, valerian

Venus: catmint, columbine, cowslip, daffodil (except yellow), daisy, damask rose, feverfew, foxglove, golden rod, orchid, primrose, rocket, rose, tansy, violet

Mars: anemone, hyssop, lesser celandine, gentian, lupin, poppy, snapdragon, tobacco plant, yellow daffodil

Jupiter: borage, eglantine, forget-me-not, geranium, houseleek, hyssop, petunia, pinks

Saturn: comfrey, cornflower, ivy, knapweed, pansy, polygonatum, willow-herb

Finally, if you wish to honour Priapus, the ancient and well-endowed god of gardens and orchards, do plant some garden rocket (*Hesperis matronalis*) in a sunny corner. Its presence there will help spread health and vigour throughout your garden.

10

Your Zodiac Angels

Good men are the stars, the planets of the ages wherein they live, and illustrate the times.

From *De Piis et Probis* by Ben Jonson

W<small>E DO</small> not live, of course, by bread alone, which is why I must now give some attention to how the zodiac can help satisfy your spiritual needs.

It can do this, I believe, in two ways. First, through the spirit beings traditionally known as angels that are associated with it, and second, by looking beyond this existence, both backwards and forwards, to consider the seven planetary lives which we must all undergo.

Let us start with the angels.

We unfortunately hear or see little of these beings nowadays, which is odd because they were once frequently encountered announcing this or heralding that. Yet their apparent absence from the world should not be taken to mean that they do not exist or that they no longer care about us, but rather that our spiritual nature has now become so corrupted that we are no longer capable of perceiving them.

For angels are still actively involved in our lives, their primary purpose being to serve as intermediaries between us and God, carrying on the one hand the deity's word to us and on the other our prayers to Him. In this respect they serve as an important link between the great religions of Christianity, Judaism and Islam, each of which, despite their many differences, acknowledges the existence of angels and recognises their divine importance.

But what exactly are angels? Quite simply they are spiritual

entities occupying a position in the hierarchy of being inter-
mediate between ourselves and God. They do not have any
form as such, yet when they choose to manifest to the psych-
ically aware they may be perceived as either handsome men
(their most frequent guise) or beautiful women, or indeed as
persons of dual sexuality, as Milton pointed out:

> For Spirits when they please
> Can either sex assume, or both; so soft
> And uncompounded is their Essence pure . . .

They wear robes of shining whiteness and their heads are sur-
rounded by a nimbus of light. And sometimes, yet by no
means always, they have one or more pairs of wings.

The name 'angel' derives from the Greek word *angelophorus*,
meaning 'messenger', and which describes as is mentioned
above, their main function, that of spiritual go-betweens who
can traverse the gulf separating our world from God.

But the situation is complicated by the fact that the term
'angel', while applied generically to all of these spiritual
creatures, is specific only to the lowest ranking of them. For
the angelic host is a hierarchy consisting of three divine
triads, each of which is divided into three grades or orders, the
first or highest triad being made up, in descending order, of
angels called seraphim, cherubim, and thrones, the second
triad of dominations, principalities, and powers, and the last
or lowest triad of virtues, archangels, and angels.

A further complication arises from the term 'archangel',
which like 'angel' is actually the name of one particular
angelic order, yet it is frequently and confusingly applied to
members of any order with a ranking above that of angel.
Thus the seraph Michael, for example, who is the ruling
prince of this highest order, and thus the most powerful angel
of all, is often called an 'archangel'.

There are believed to be only four seraphim, who are
known as the archangels of light, love, and fire, and in keeping with their number they are said to possess, at least when
they manifest on earth, four faces and six wings (see Figure 1).

Their role in heaven is apparently, to stand by the throne of God chanting the trisagion – 'Holy, holy, holy'.

Figure 1. A Seraphim

Cherubs or cherubim are often mistakenly portrayed by artists as plump, winged infants, but in fact these powerful archangels manifest as large beings with four faces and either four or six wings. They are, like the seraphim, angels of light and also of glory, although their main function in Heaven is to keep the celestial records. Hence they are remarkably wise and knowledgeable, characteristics that would sit uncomfortably in an infantile form.

The order of thrones makes up the third rank of the highest angelic triad. There are a total of 70 of these archangels and they too possess four faces and also four wings. Thrones are known for their steadfastness and for their loyalty to God, traits which are necessary for their function, which is to ensure that divine justice is meted out to each of us according to how we live our lives.

The middle-ranking angelic triad of dominations, principalities, and powers, is made up of archangels whose functions are regulatory and protective. They normally manifest possessing two faces and four wings, and their countenances are beautiful but sombre, as befits their role as guardians.

Dominations, the highest ranking order of this group, are concerned with managing the activities of the angels, which are the lowest, yet by far the most numerous, grade. The principalities, by contrast, concern themselves with watching over our leaders and with ensuring the continuance of religious belief, while the powers guard our world against its sudden overthrow by fallen angels or demons.

The angelic beings comprising the lowest triad, which is made up of virtues, archangels, and angels, normally manifest in a recognisably human form, that is, with one head and face, and if they reveal themselves with wings, it is the traditional single pair. These angels have the greatest direct contact with us, for they function as guardians, guides, and messengers.

The virtues are said not only to give grace and valour to those who are deserving of them, but to work miracles. Hence they are the spirits to whom one should appeal when divine help is urgently required. The archangels themselves, of which different accounts give a minimum of four or a maximum of twelve, although seven is the number most commonly suggested, are chiefly concerned with asking God to forgive those who fail to learn despite having opportunity to do so, and also to request that happy hearts be given to those who are righteous. Yet on occasions they bear God's tidings directly to mankind.

And lastly, the angels proper have a role that is primarily

one of communication, which they may fulfil by bringing, or appearing in, dreams, or alternatively by direct revelation, as happened, for example, when news of Jesus' birth was given to the shepherds by one of the angelic host appearing to them. Additionally, the angels serve as our own individual guardians, as one presides over each of us from the cradle to the grave.

There are higher angels associated with each of the planets and with all of the zodiac signs. The two that are most important to you are the angel of your Sun sign planetary ruler and that of your zodiac Sun sign itself. Yet because there is by no means complete agreement among the authorities as to the correct names of these angels, I shall note the commonest alternative, if any, to the principal one given.

The angel of the Sun is Michael (or Uriel); the angel of the Moon is Gabriel; of Mercury, Raphael; of Venus, Anael (sometimes spelled Aniel); of Mars, Samael (or Camael); of Jupiter, Zadkiel (or Barchiel); and of Saturn, Cassiel (or Zaphiel). These angels also govern the seven days of the week.

Because each of these divine beings belongs to a higher order than the angels proper, they may be termed archangels, although Michael, Gabriel and Raphael are all seraphim, the highest angelic grade.

While it is extremely unlikely that your planetary angel will communicate with you directly, he can and will intercede for you with God himself if your need is great enough. Your prayers are most likely to be heard if you make them on the weekday belonging to your ruling planet, particularly if you also choose the hour which it rules (see Chapter Eight).

The angels governing the zodiac signs all have a higher rank than archangel, which means that your own zodiac angel will probably never appear to you directly. Yet he is aware of you and is interested in your welfare, for it was his job to guide your soul into the body it now occupies and to bring you both into the world during his zodiac period. He naturally desires and earnestly hopes that you will lead a life that is worthy of your existence, although he is not normally permitted to intervene directly and warn you if you are not. In this respect we are all responsible for our actions and must take the consequences if we do wrong and let our zodiac angel down. However, like the planetary archangels, your zodiac archangel can and will bring your prayers directly to God's notice if you call on him by name. He is perhaps most sensitive to your appeals during your birth period, yet you will never be ignored if your need is genuine.

The angel of Aries is named Malahidael (or Machidiel), who is a ruling prince of the order of thrones. If Malahidael is invoked through magic, he has the power, it is said, to bring to the magician any woman (or man) he (or she) desires.

The angel of Taurus is named Asmodiel (or Asmodel), who was once a very high angel, being a chief of the order of cherubim. Yet having taken part aeons ago in an angelic walk-out of Heaven, his rank is now lower and somewhat indeterminate, although he is not, as some mischief-makers would have, the demon of punishment.

The angel of Gemini is called Ambriel, who is a prince of the order of thrones. The 12th hour of the night belongs to him.

The angel of Cancer is named Muriel (sometimes spelled as Murriel), who is a ruler of the order of dominations, and thus a high-ranking angel. He is also the guardian of the third hour of the day.

The angel of Leo is named Verchiel, who is one of the rulers of the order of powers.

The angel of Virgo is called Hamaliel and he is one of the rulers of the order of virtues.

The angel of Libra is named Zuriel. He is a prince of the order of principalities, and one of his functions is to aid women in childbirth. He also has the power, which seems to be less frequently used nowadays, to cure human stupidity.

The angel of Scorpio is Barchiel (or Barbiel), who is one of the seven archangels. Barchiel not only has jurisdiction over lightning, but also over one's luck at gambling.

The angel of Sagittarius is Advachiel (or Adnachiel), who is a prince of the order of powers.

The angel of Capricorn is called Hamael, who is either a ruler of the order of thrones or a chief of the order of principalities. His special power is that he can protect you against the forces of evil.

The angel of Aquarius is named Cambiel. He is a prince of the order of dominations and the guardian of the ninth hour of the day.

Lastly, the angel of Pisces is the same as that of Scorpio, namely Barchiel, the only angel to govern two zodiac signs. He resides in the Second Heaven, and some would have it that he is also ruler of the planet Jupiter.

These eleven archangels preside over numerous angels belonging to that order and which are the 'foot soldiers' of the twelve signs, serving as they do as personal guardian angels to each of us. These lowermost entities of the angelic hierarchy watch over us, record our good deeds and our disgraceful acts, and try, where possible, to give us good counsel and guard us from harm. Yet they cannot save us from our fate, which is royally signposted in the heavens at the moment of our birth, and whose broad outline is determined, for better or worse, by the type of life we have led in our past lives.

11

Planetary Lives

Thus Aristotle's soul, of old that was
May now be damned to animate as ass;
Or in this very house, for ought we know,
Is doing painful penance in some beau.

From a comedy prologue by William Congreve

THERE IS growing evidence from a variety of sources that the life which each of us now leads is not the only one that we shall know. In fact we may not only have lived before but will probably do so again.

This doctrine, which is called reincarnation or metempsychosis, is based upon the premise that our bodies are composed of two temporarily joined parts, one of which is physical and mortal, the other spiritual and immortal. When the first dies, the second is released back into the spirit world, and then sometime later, upon having remained 'in spirit' to rest and to take stock of its earthly experiences (which may include a period of mourning or even penance for its wrongdoing), is directed by a zodiac sign angel into another physical body and is thereby reborn into the world.

Some believers in reincarnation claim that the spirit body or soul not only takes up residence in a series of different human bodies, but may, at least on occasions, inhabit the physical form of other creatures, even plants. The Greek philosopher Empedocles, for example, claimed to have remembered past lives spent as a bird, a fish, and a bush, as well as other human existences.

Reincarnation is a very ancient belief, which may have

149

originated in India, where it is still widely accepted today. The Indians explain it by saying that although the soul's true home lies in the realm of the divine and that its ultimate destination or goal is union with God, it cannot remain in the spirit world or achieve its objective until it has lived in the physical world and experienced the vicissitudes and temptations of earthly existence.

Unfortunately, while in the human body, the soul often falls prey to those temptations. When this happens, it builds up a spiritual debt known as *karma*, which must be worked off before it can progress further. And should some or all of the karmic debt remain when the body dies, the soul is then automatically reincarnated into another body, within which it has the possibility to either erase that debt or, by continuing to live immorally and wickedly, to foolishly add to it.

By their position within the zodiac and by their relationship to one another, the planets symbolise the nature of the physical bed or body into which the reincarnated soul is planted. They represent, in other words, its strengths and its weaknesses, and it is by being aware of these, that we can all, if sufficiently wise, plot a better course through life and so advance ourselves spiritually.

It now seems likely that every soul must live through at least one cycle of seven planetary lives (each one of which takes its primary characteristics from the planet after which it is named) before union with God is possible. In this way our souls are not only exposed to the types of temptation peculiar to each planet, these being lust, pride, greed, vanity, sloth, envy, and anger, known as the seven deadly sins, but are given the opportunity to resist each of them and so win spiritual grace.

The cycle of planetary lives, so far as can be ascertained, apparently follows this order: the first is the Moon life, the second the Mercury life, the third the Venus life, the fourth the Sun life, the fifth the Mars life, the sixth the Jupiter life, and the last and seventh the Saturn life.

This system of seven helps explain the wide variations of needs, disposition, and craving, that exist between people, as well as accounting for the different degrees of hope, optimism, despair, and resignation, that they show.

Hence during the course of your present planetary cycle your soul will reside in a total of seven different physical bodies, although because it needs to experience life as undergone by both sexes, in some of these lives you will be a man, in others a woman. In general, but not always, the planetary lives alternate their genders. Hence if you are a woman now, you were probably a man in your last incarnation and may be a man again in your next. The reverse applies if you are a man now. Yet as we can see from the example given later, regarding the past lives of the philosopher Pythagoras, such regular alternation of the sexes does not always occur.

There is apparently no fixed length to a planetary cycle. This will vary according to the length of the individual lives and the length of the time spent between death and the next incarnation. But obviously, if each life lasts an average of sixty years and if reincarnation happens more or less immediately, the entire cycle will take approximately 420 years. However, because the soul will normally need to restore its energies, absorb its experiences, and wait to greet the souls of loved ones who die after it, in between each planetary life, the cycle is likely to be longer. If we take 30 years as being the probable average interval of time between each life, and if the lives themselves last an average of, say, sixty years, then the cycle itself will take about 600 years.

When your soul finally completes its long journey from your first planetary life to the end of your last, it will know intimately every emotion, every feeling, every desire. It will, it is hoped, have confronted and resisted its lusts, its ambitions, its hates and its vices. It will certainly have had every opportunity to grow, to love, to give and to mature.

Your zodiac birth sign is the key to which planetary life you are currently living through, as the planetary ruler of your Sun sign is the same planet as that governing your present life. This in turn will tell you if you are a new, medium-term, or old soul. Further, it will enable you to determine which of the seven deadly sins you are most likely to find troublesome. And

forewarned is forearmed. Such knowledge may help you to resist your worst impulses and safeguard the purity of your soul.

The list below gives all the relevant details:

Zodiac birth sign	Planetary life	Sin you must guard against
Cancer	(1) Moon	Envy
Gemini, Virgo	(2) Mercury	Vanity
Taurus, Libra	(3) Venus	Lust
Leo	(4) Sun	Pride
Aries, Scorpio	(5) Mars	Anger
Pisces, Sagittarius	(6) Jupiter	Greed
Capricorn, Aquarius	(7) Saturn	Sloth

Only those souls that have committed great crimes during one
or more of their lives will perhaps need to undergo yet another
cycle of planetary lives. It is very doubtful, for instance, if the
souls of those Mars life individuals like Josef Stalin, Papadoc
Duvalier, Josef Goebbels and Chairman Mao (who were all
born under Aries), will be able to expunge their enormous
karmic debts during the remaining two lives of their present
planetary cycles. They must expect therefore to be reborn
many times, probably into lives that at first inflict much pain,
suffering, and humiliation on them, but which then give them
the opportunity to redress their awful wrongs by caring for
others.

However, it is pertinent to ask why God should create a
soul and then force it to undergo a series of life experiences?
The answer perhaps lies in the fact that the soul is a fragment
of the divine. Thus when it resides in a physical body it contributes something of benefit to both it and the world, while
gaining knowledge and experience that, once its planetary
cycle is completed, is absorbed into the 'bank' or 'library' of
universal understanding. In certain planetary lives, for instance, some souls are able radically to influence and improve
the thoughts and actions of others. Holy men and the pure in

heart, for example, are often living through their last, or Saturn life, eschewing as they do bodily or material temptations to show love, care, and understanding to others, and to help improve the lot of all. They may also be men and women of great intellect who help mankind through their discoveries. Some also are ascetics and psychics. Five such Saturn people are Cicero, Francis Bacon, Emmanuel Swedenborg, Abraham Lincoln, and Charles Darwin.

The ancient philosopher Pythagoras, who is most famous for his discovery that the square on the hypotenuse of a right-angled triangle is equal to the sum of the squares on the other two sides, was probably living through his last or Saturn life. Like Empedocles, he claimed to be able to remember having lived before. In one life, he said, he was a man called Euphorbus, who fought at the siege of Troy. This was presumably his Mars life. In another, his previous or Jupiter life, he was a fisherman named Hermotimus. He also recalled being a man named Aethalides, who Pythagorus said, was the son of the god Hermes or Mercury, which suggests that it was his Mercury life.

Great things may be done by those living through earlier planetary lives, if they are able to resist the particular temptation or deadly sin of that life. Thus Mahatma Gandhi, who was born under Libra, was living through his Venus life, which is typically plagued by lust, but managed successfully to master his sexual yearnings, became celibate and went on to become a sage and the guiding light of the Indian Independence movement.

However, you must also take note of the planetary ruler of your rising or ascending sign because this will signify the other area of wrongdoing that may get you into moral trouble. Hence if you were born, say, under Leo but have Capricorn as your rising sign, then you might be troubled by sloth as well as by Leo pride. And obviously, those with the same Sun sign and rising sun will be doubly tempted by the sin associated with their single planetary ruler. They will have the hardest job of all of staying on the straight and narrow.

If you would like to know the type of animal into which you

Planetary life	Animal types it includes
1) Moon	Most aquatic creatures, and all land-living crustacea (e.g. wood-lice), molluscs (a group which includes slugs and snails), and adult amphibians. Seals, and porcine mammals.
2) Mercury	Monkeys and most apes; foxes; squirrels and other arboreal mammals; all snakes, and most birds.
3) Venus	Most herbivorous mammals; earthworms and other annelids; dogs; also doves, pigeons, and sparrows.
4) Sun	Cats, lions, tigers, and other feline mammals; jackals; hens, eagles, mynahs, sparrowhawks, and vultures; all bees and butterflies.
5) Mars	Most carnivorous mammals; sheep; lobsters, tortoises, and turtles; all spiders, scorpions, ticks and mites; also wasps, hornets and mosquitoes.
6) Jupiter	Ocean-living fish and most aquatic mammals (e.g. whales and dolphins); horses and oxen; and ducks, flamingos, swans and storks.
7) Saturn	Most reptiles and insects; goats and donkeys; baboons and gorillas; and also crows, macaws and owls.

may be reincarnated into your next planetary life, the list shown above will serve as a useful guide. Those who are in their last or Saturn life, which includes all born under the zodiac signs of Capricorn and Aquarius, should examine the animals listed for the Moon. They may become one of these if they have the misfortune to undergo another cycle of planetary lives.

It is of course debatable if such a transformation should be regarded as a punishment or a reward. It is true that those who spend their lives treading on others could be justly served by being made to undergo an existence as some small and insignificant creature, which could be squashed underfoot at any time, yet because animals live in a state of natural innocence, uncorrupted as they are by human desires, then perhaps we may conclude that to join their number is a blessing.

If any one of these animal types appears regularly in your dreams, it may mean that you were such a creature in a previous life. This may also be the case if you love any particular type of animal, for your loving feelings may stem from subconscious memories of the happiness you had as that animal. However, should you have a phobia about any particular animal type, it may be that the animal in question ate you or was otherwise responsible for your death, in either a human or animal form, in an earlier existence.

Afterword

And as those errant planets in their distinct orbs have their
several motions, sometimes direct, stationary, retrograde, in
apogee, perigee, oriental, occidental, combust, feral, free, and
as our astrologers will, have their fortitudes and debilities, by
reason of those good and bad irradiations, conferred to each
other's site in the heavens, in their terms, houses, case, detri-
ments, etc. So we rise and fall in this world, ebb and flow, in
and out, reared and dejected, lead a troublesome life, subject
to many accidents and casualities of fortunes, variety of passions, infirmities as well as from ourselves as others.

From *Remedies of all Manners of Discontents* by Robert Burton

POSITIONED AS we are so close to the end of the millennium,
which necessarily creates all manner of hopes for, and
anxieties about, the future, it is perhaps relevant to consider
what astrology can tell us about the way ahead. Do we stand
on the brink of a new and better age? – or are the years to
come going to be worse, if that is possible, than those we have
recently experienced?

The end of this millennium is different from the last as it
will approximately coincide with the end of what is known as
an *astrological age*. The latter is a lengthy period of time that
takes its name from the zodiac constellation in which the Sun
is placed at the spring equinox, and as the Sun is presently situated in Pisces then, we are living at the tail end of the Age of
Pisces. Ahead of us lies, in the not too distant future, the Age
of Aquarius, which explains why the cast of the 1960s musical
Hair! sang, 'This is the dawning of the Age of Aquarius.'

Afterword

The existence of changing astrological ages derives from two unusual features of the spring equinox (and which are also shared by the autumn equinox and the two solstices), the first being, that it is moving, and the second that it moves in a retrograde, or backward, manner through the zodiac. This is why the coming age will not be the Age of Aries.

However, the astute reader might very reasonably wonder why, considering that the spring equinox takes place in the northern hemisphere on March 20th, when the Sun is supposedly lodged in Aries, we are now living in the Age of Pisces? Shouldn't we really be approaching the end of the Age of Aries and looking ahead to the Age of Pisces?

We would be, if the Sun was actually placed at the 'first point' or start of Aries on March 20th. But in fact that was the Sun's position at the spring equinox of 140 BC when the Greek astronomer Hipparchus (died 125 BC) discovered that the equinoxes are not fixed. Ever since, in order to keep the equinoxes and solstices at their same position in the calendar, the spring equinox has been assigned to March 20th, notwithstanding the fact that the Sun is now approaching the 'first point' of Pisces on that date. Had this system not been adopted the equinoxes and solstices would gradually shift backwards through the entire calendar, which would mean, for example, that in roughly four thousand years' time the spring equinox would take place on December 22nd, the present date of the winter solstice!

The placement of the spring equinox in Aries back in Hipparchus's time is the reason why Aries became the first sign of the zodiac. But, correctly speaking, its position of primacy was superseded by Pisces in about 100 BC when the spring equinox entered that sign and Aries in turn became the second zodiac sign. Similarly, within 65 years Aquarius will become the first zodiac sign, while Pisces will slip into second, and Aries into third, place. However, it is doubtful if our astrologers will pay any attention to the realities of the changing sky, but will continue to practise their art as usual with their heads firmly buried in the sand.

The precession of the equinoxes is caused by the 'wobble' of the Earth's axis, which is brought about by the gravitational pull of the Sun and the Moon. The 'wobble' takes approximately 25,900 years to complete one revolution, during which time the spring equinox moves backward through all of the twelve zodiac signs. This long period is known as the Great Year. Furthermore, if we divide 25,900 by twelve we arrive at the time it takes for the spring equinox to pass through each zodiac sign, which is 2,158 years. This is the length of an astrological age, when the zodiac sign through which the spring equinox is preceding confers or imposes its character, for good or ill, on the Earth and upon those who live on it. This is why, for the last two thousand years or so, our world has been subject to all the uncertainties, religious fervour, cruelty and paranoia of watery Pisces; whereas soon, however, it will be governed by cool, unemotional and objective Aquarius. A far better way of life may thus be enjoyed by our descendants.

Because the Age of Pisces started in about 100 BC it will end, again approximately, in AD 2058, when the Age of Aquarius will begin. Going even further back in time, we find that the Age of Leo began, coincidentally enough, at the end of the last Ice Age about 10,890 years BC and continued until about 8,732 BC. It was followed by the Age of Cancer (c. 8,732 – 6,574 BC), which in turn was succeeded by the Age of Gemini (c. 6,574 – 4,416 BC), the Age of Taurus (c. 4,416 – 2,258 BC), the Age of Aries (c. 2,258 – 100 BC), and the Age of Pisces (100 BC – AD 2,058), which brings us up to our own time. The Age of Aquarius, by contrast, will continue until AD 4216, long after we are all dead and forgotten.

We are presently, of course, in a period of transition, in which the influences of Pisces is loosening its grip and giving way, protestingly and ungraciously, to that of Aquarius. So we must expect, as we are indeed seeing, the countries and peoples of the world to experience further instability and upset, which will almost certainly be accompanied by similar disasters in the natural world. Yet Aquarius has already begun imposing its character on us, and is doing it at a steadily accelerating rate. After all, Aquarius is traditionally linked with aeroplanes and space flight, electricity and electronics, computation and technology, and nuclear fission, all of which have been developed in the 20th century. It is also associated with democracy, freedom and humanitarian beliefs, which have likewise spread their benefits to more of the world's population in recent years. These characteristics will continue to oust those of Pisces, until the Age of Aquarius imposes its own brighter disposition wholly on our world, improving the lot of every man and woman. Aquarius is the most far-sighted and individualistic of the twelve signs, and it will encourage clearer thinking, more rational behaviour, and kinder hearts to replace the unstable emotions, self-hatred, rampant greed and licentiousness, and the long, dark shadows of the Age of Pisces.

Index